THE
GUILTLESS GOURMET

LOW IN FAT, CHOLESTEROL, SALT, SUGAR, CALORIES

Judy Gilliard & Joy Kirkpatrick, RD

Text & cover design: Terry Dugan Design
Typesetting: Dahl & Curry
Printing: Mike Beard & Assoc.

Diabetes Center, Inc.
Minneapolis, Minnesota
Copyright © 1987 by The Guiltless Gourmet Partnership
Published by Diabetes Center, Inc.
P.O. Box # 739
Wayzata, Minnesota 55391

Library of Congress Cataloging-in-Publication Data

Gillard, Judy.
     The guiltless gourmet.

     (The Wellness and nutrition library)
     Includes Index.
     1. Low-fat diet—Recipes.   2. Salt-free diet—Recipes.
3. Low-calorie diet—Recipes.   I. Kirkpatrick, Joy.
II. Title.   III. Series.
RM237.7.G55 1987   641.5'63   87-24521
ISBN 0-937721-23-9 (pbk.)

Printed in the United States of America

Dedicated to: Ken Garett, Ph.D.—for his support and helping to keep it all together.

ACKNOWLEDGMENTS

We owe thanks to many friends and supporters—all of whom we hardly have room to list. But a few people deserve special recognition.

Illustration: Teri (Flaun) Gilliard

Taste Testers: Karen Stickel, David Dean, Don Keagle, Diane Durham, Karl Reimann, Angela Davis, Lloyd Green, Jiim Harris, Louis Pontarelli, Marlene Schweit, Kathy Richerdson.

Inspiration: Jeanne Jones, Cris Newport, R.D., T. Alyn King
Help and Recipe Analysis: Bill Kasal

Our Title: Edyth Lawson.

Photos: Art and Cheryl Coleman.
Special thanks to Terry and Sharon Adams
Dick Huettner and Gary Goodwin of Ralphs Markets, and to Cafarelli's and the Desert Wharf for their cooperation.
                                                    Judy Gilliard
                                                    Joy Kirkpatrick R.D.

Preface

One wonders, as one picks up another nutrition and balanced-diet book, is another book on the subject really needed? Just who are these dedicated-diet people? Do they really know what they are saying? And, in the end, does it matter?

Of course, it matters—at least to a physician who has seen a continuous stream of patients afflicted with diabetes, obesity, atherosclerotic diseases; who has witnessed the complications, the tragic end results and the attendant frustrations; who know that the answer comes not from stop-gap measures which attempt to turn the tide against foregone failures, but rather from prevention—from honest attempts to stay the atherosclerotic process before the ravages of time.

Fortunately, there is a new nutritional awareness and it is making its presence known and beginning to take hold. So long as we continue to face the unacceptable frequency of strokes, of heart attacks, of blindness, infections, social stigma and the other myriad of ills which accompany hypertension, diabetes and obesity, there cannot be too many diet manuals and nutritional approaches. But one has to choose carefully and wisely.

In "The Guiltless Gourmet," one finds a gem. Both eminently useful and understandable, this book has been co-authored by a synergistic team. Joy Kirkpatrick has more than a decade of direct patient experience in her role as a Registered Dietitian—most adept at plying her trade, fielding questions and converting the complex morass of numbers and nutrients into simple, lucid recipes. Along with Judy Gilliard, a professional restaurant consultant and instructor, what we find in "The Guiltless Gourmet" is not only a highly credible and entertaining effort, but we are only at the beginning.

Based upon your newly gained knowledge, you will be able to create an infinite variety of your own individual gourmet treats. Delectable *and* nutritious. Most enjoyable—for good luck, good health and good appetite. What more could you want?

Richard J. Mahler, MD

Chief, Metabolism and Endocrinology
Director, Diabetes Program
Eisenhower Medical Center
Rancho Mirage, California

Introduction

We bring you good news, and more good news. For as a nation, we are fortunately becoming more health conscious. We are beginning to realize that the first, and most important step in improving and maintaining our good health begins with diet.

There is a simple equation for this. The right foods in the right quantities help assure a healthy body and an alert mind—with the essential benefits of looking and feeling our best. What could be more desirable?

Undeniably for many of us, we find our lifestyles rushed and complicated. But nutrition need not take a back seat to our jobs, family commuting and business commitments. With a basic understanding of sound nutritional principles, healthy eating habits can readily become a way of life.

To help speed you along this tantalizing trail of "guiltless gourmet" dining, we have assembled sections on breakfast, brunch and lunch, salads, main dishes, sauces, desserts and specialty coffees. Representative items include home-baked bread, rolls, waffles, pancakes, quiches, tacos, fish, poultry, meat and lamb dishes, spinach, fruit and lettuce salads with specialty dressings, sauces, chutney, cheesecakes, Black Forest cake, mousses, puddings, Expresso and hot chocolate Cappucino.

"The Guiltless Gourmet" provides simple nutritional information, plus recipes, menus, charts and hints which you will find convenient and fun to use. These recipes have been especially designed to be simple, inexpensive, low in calories, fat, cholesterol and salt, yet high in fiber and nutritional value, tasty and pleasing to the eye as well as the palate.

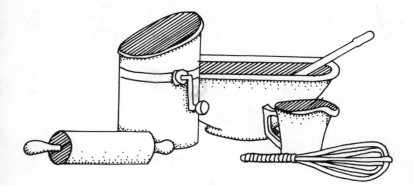

Contents

The Basic Four and More....

For years we have been raised with the basic four food groups as our first introduction into nutrition. Indeed, the basic four (fruits and vegetables, meat and protein foods, dairy products, grains and cereals) continue to be a valid teaching tool, even while a more sophisticated audience has demanded more information.

Americans are generally quite calorie-conscious. But often this is not enough. The nutritional value of calories may not add up to a balanced diet. Calories are the end result of the amount of foods eaten from the three major nutrient groups: carbohydrates, proteins and fats. Other nutrient groups—vitamins, minerals and water—contain no calories, but are very important in the actual value of the foods we eat. Another category—that of fiber—may or may not be considered a nutrient. However, fiber has been shown to be important in the overall diet.

A LITTLE SIMPLE, NUTRITION-WISE MATHEMATICS

Carbohydrates contain 4 calories per gram:
   I teaspoon of sugar contains 4 grams of carbohydrate
                          so
         4 grams X 4 calories = 16 calories

Fats contain 9 calories per gram:
          I teaspoon of fat contains 5 grams of fat
                          so
         5 grams X 9 calories = 45 calories

 Proteins contain 4 calories per gram:
I ounce of protein contains approximately 7 grams of protein
                          so
      7 grams X 4 calories = 28 calories of protein

   However...all protein sources we eat also contain measurable amounts of fat, too. This means that one ounce of lean meat has part protein and part fat. The fat and protein must be considered together when figuring calories.

A better example would be:
I ounce of protein (lean meat) contains 7 grams of protein
                                          + 3 grams of fat.
7 grams of protein X 4 calories per gram = 28 calories
 + 3 grams of fat X 9 calories per gram = 27 calories
   _____
   or I ounce of lean meat = 55 calories

(Even for a simple mathematician, 7 grams = 3 grams only adds up to a total of 10 grams. The rest of the weight of I ounce, or 30 grams of lean meat, is water!)

CARBOHYDRATES
   While all carbohydrates have the same caloric value the sources

are very different. There are two major categories of carbohydrates—sugars and starches.

Sugars are also referred to as simple sugar or refined sugar. They include white table sugar, brown and raw sugar, molasses, syrups, corn syrup, jams, jellies, desserts, candies and all fruits and fruit juices. While fruit and fruit juices are more nutritious than other forms of sugar, their major composition is of simple sugar.

Starches are such foods as cereals, grains, potatoes, corn, peas, rice and pasta. These foods are often thought to be fattening. Nothing could be further from the truth! As long as complex starches do not have fat added to them, they are not fattening. In fact, they are the substances of which the bulk of our diets should be comprised. Surprised! Try it and you'll see for yourself.

PROTEINS

Protein foods include all meats, fish, poultry, eggs, cheese and to a certain degree, dried beans and peas. But, remember: all protein foods contain fat which raises the calories significantly. Our bodies do not have a specific requirement for protein per se. Rather, they require a certain number of amino acids—the building blocks or components of protein—that are derived from the protein we eat. The actual amount of protein foods our bodies require is often less than half what the average person eats. What happens to the rest? It turns to fat and is stored in areas we would rather not have it!

FATS

Fats include butter, margarine, all oils, nuts, bacon, avocado, mayonnaise, olives, cream and sour cream. Fats are very concentrated sources of energy (calories). They are at the top of the list as far as foods we should limit or avoid. Did you know that a pie or a cake is not especially high in sugar calories? Sugar has only 4 calories per gram. Pie or cake has most of its calories in fat.

MILK

Milk has not yet been mentioned. It is an interesting combination of carbohydrates, proteins and fats.

	CHO	PRO	FAT	CALORIES
8 oz. whole milk contains	12 g	8 g	8 g	150
8 oz. lowfat milk (2% fat)	12	8	5	120
8 oz. nonfat milk (less than 1% fat)	12	8	t	90

So, milk is a good source of carbohydrates and proteins. But it can be high in fat, depending on the type you choose. Note that yogurt products have the same composition as the type of milk they are made from (without the addition of fruits and other flavorings.)

NOTE: All recipes presented in this book have been nutritionally analyzed by computer. The "exchange values" listed have been estimated according to the amount of carbohydrate, protein and fat contained in each recipe.

Kitchen Basics

Keeping your kitchen well-stocked saves time as well as money. You can take advantage of store specials and sales by buying more than you need of canned fruits, vegetables, broths and bouillons, etc. Frozen vegetables have a storage life of between three and six months, as do most meats, poultry and fish, if they are wrapped tightly for the freezer. Pastas such as spaghetti, macaroni and noodles will do very well for months in a dry "pantry" area, as long as they, too, are kept tightly wrapped. Whole grain pastas and flour products should preferably be stored in the refrigerator or freezer.

Some recommended items to have in your kitchen or pantry always on hand are:

DAIRY:
nonfat milk
corn-oil margarine
eggs
parmesan cheese
low-fat, or part-skim
cheeses
low-fat or nonfat yogurt
sour cream

PERISHABLES:
lemons
parsley
whole grain bread or rolls
carrots
onions
potatoes
salad greens
tomatoes
garlic
shallots
celery
fresh fruits and vegetables in season

CANNED GOODS:
whole tomatoes
tomato paste
tomato puree
chicken stock
water chestnuts
evaporated skimmed milk

BOTTLED ITEMS:
olive oil
corn oil
apple cider vinegar, or
white wine vinegar, or
red wine vinegar, or
rice wine vinegar
dijon-style mustard
red or green chili salsa
Tabasco sauce
Worcestershire sauce
mayonnaise (low calorie preferred

DRY INGREDIENTS:

Flour:	Equal™
unbleached	brown rice
whole wheat	bulgar
whole wheat pastry flour	beans
unbleached pastry flour	noodles
baking soda	macaroni
baking powder	spaghetti
cream of tartar	barley
fructose	Butter Buds®

A variety of frozen fruits and vegetables also comes in very handy. We use frozen apple and orange juice concentrates in cooking and as natural, fruit-based sweetners, too.

MAKE LIFE EASIER IN THE KITCHEN BY HAVING

Measuring cups, 2 sets
Pyrex or plastic liquid measuring cup, 1-, 2- and 8-cup sizes.
diet scale
oven thermometer
timer
colander
salad spin dryer
knives
   chef's
   paring
   boning
   bread
   tomato
sharpening stone
sharpening steel
vegetable peeler
apple corer and slicer
2 rubber spatulas
all-purpose kitchen shears
mortar and pestle
pepper mill
nutmeg grinder
juicer (electic or hand)
blender

food processor (unnecessary if you have a blender, but very helpful, so have a kitchen savings fund)
whisks, small, medium and large
wooden spoons
bowls
    stainless steel
    4- to 10-piece glass mixing set
    wood salad bowl
waffle iron (nonstick surface)
skillets
    several sizes of well seasoned cast iron as they give a
        good, even heat....
2 or 3 non-stick skillets
enamel coated saucepans, small and medium or stainless steel
4-quart dutch oven
10-quart dutch oven, enamel coated
large spaghetti pot
steamer
baking dishes: 9 x 9, 9 x 13, glass or metal with nonstick surface
quiche pans, 2 8-inch
molds
jelly roll pan, 10- x 15-inch
3-in-1 springform pan
muffin tin
flour sifter

There are a few items that are more costly, but if you cook a lot, you can make it easier and save hours of preparation by being well-equipped. So, start a kitchen fund, put a little money aside whenever you can for such things. When making major purchases for your kitchen, spend a little more for quality items that will last 20 to 30 years!
    *food processor
    *Kitchen Aid or large Mixmaster
    *coffee grinder

Hints About Ingredients

Chicken Broth—For ease in calculations we used regular canned broth. It can be found in any grocery store. For those on sodium-restricted diets, you can use chicken broth without added salt. You can find it in the health food or natural food section at your market. When using low-sodium broth, you will have less sodium in your recipe than the amount we have listed. Incidentally, if you keep a can or two in the refrigerator, it will be very easy to remove the small amount of fat that is in most canned broths.

Tomato Products—We used regular canned items—some have salt added, some do not. For a lower salt diet, we suggest you try the lower salt version of canned tomato products that are now available.

Soy Sauce—This item is very high in sodium. It is used in moderation in a few recipes, but if you need a lower salt diet we suggest you omit it.

Brown Rice—We have used two different varieties—long grain and short grain. Short grain is more sticky and works best for the Brown Rice Pudding. Long grain gives a better texture to the casserole-type recipes. You can interchange them if you don't want to buy two different types—the choice is yours.

Bulgar—This is generally available in most supermarkets. It is whole wheat that has been roasted, dried and cracked. If you can't find it in the market, we suggest you try a health food store or even an Italian deli where pasta and the like can be found in bulk.

Apple Juice Concentrate—This is frozen, canned apple juice concentrate found in the freezer section at your market. It could be called a "natural" sweetner, but alas, it is a simple sugar and should be used with care.

Flours—We have used four types, unbleached, unbleached pastry flour, whole wheat and whole wheat pastry flour. Unbleached pastry is used if an item is lighter or more delicate.

Unprocessed Bran—This is also known as miller's bran. It is available in most markets and/or health food stores. It is fairly inexpensive and adds fiber to the diet.

Tuna and Salmon—We used canned, water packed and drained and rinsed it well. It still will have a fair amount of sodium in it, though. So, if you're on a very low-salt diet, you should use the type without any salt added.

Cheeses—We use ricotta, Farmers and parmesan. When buying ricotta cheese be sure to buy part-skim. Farmers cheese is a low fat cheese with a mild flavor and good consistency. Parmesan cheese adds a lot of flavor for the small amount that is used in various recipes. You can buy it already grated or grate your own. Remember, nearly ALL cheeses are moderately high to very high in fat and salt, so we have used them sparingly.

Cocoa—We found that imported cocoa powder gave a smoother flavor to the chocolate items. It can usually be found in the gourmet or imported food section of your market.

Vinegar—We used several different vinegars in our recipes. Most are readily available in the market. You may, however, need to special order, mail order or find a speciality store that carries the fruit vinegars such as the raspberry vinegar used in the *Poppy Seed Dressing*. They aren't absolutely necessary, but do add a lovely, delicate flavor.

Equal (NutraSweet™)—This is a relatively new low-calorie sweetner on the market. It is not saccharine-based as most other sugar substitutes are; rather, it is made from two naturally occurring amino acids and is used commercially under the name of NutraSweet™, or Aspartame. NutraSweet is 200 times sweeter than sugar so very little is needed for sweetening. Consumers buy it under the label of Equal which is NutraSweet™ and a very small amount of lactose so each individual packet contains 4 calories. At this point it is safe to say that Equal can be used in moderation by diabetics and those on weight loss diets who are trying to cut their sugar consumption. Two disadvantages of the product at this time are: it is more costly than most sugar substitutes and it cannot be used in baking or cooking involving high temperatures because it loses its sweetening power. For this reason—when we have used Equal in any of our recipes we say to add it *after* the item is cooked.

Butter Buds®—A very low-fat substitute for butter or margarine that has the real flavor of butter but without the calories. We have used it in various recipes to add the flavor of butter, yet keep the fat calories low. If you buy Butter Buds + y at your market, read the package brochures carefully, then experiment on your own.

Spices and herbs add a marvelous sparkle to dishes. If you desire to cut down on salt intake, they can be used in combination with or instead of salt, both in cooking and at the table. It's fun to experiment with the different aromas, tastes and hues spices and herbs lend to everyday or glamorous dishes. But, a word of caution: use them sparingly at first. It's always better to add than to try to subtract.

Herbs are usually the fresh or dried leaves of plants. They can be cultivated in a small window or outdoor garden; dried, chopped and frozen for use year-round.

Spices are from the bark, root, fruits or berries of plants. They are best purchased in small quantities, since a crushed or dried spice can lose flavor rapidly.

A few "starter" herb combinations are represented here, but use your own imagination and family's taste judgment to combine your own.

Basic Herb and Spice List

ALLSPICE: combines the flavors of cinnamon, cloves and nutmeg. It is best used in fruits, desserts, cranberry sauce and on cottage cheese.

BASIL: adds sparkle to all vegetables and soups. Excellent on tomatoes and in tomato sauces. It is used in most Italian dishes. Has the capacity to sweeten dishes.

CAYENNE, RED PEPPER AND CHILI POWDER: hot or spicy peppers. These add sparkle and zip to cheese sauces, chili dishes, vegetable soups and casseroles, barbecued poultry and meats, scrambled or baked egg dishes.

CELERY SEED: the seed of the celery plant. It adds a pungent scent and characteristic flavor of celery. Good used as salad or vegetable seasoning, in vegetable casseroles and soups.

CINNAMON: a sweet, aromatic, ground bark from a relative of the laurel tree. Cinnamon sweetens baked goods, is excellent in any dish prepared with apples, squash or pumpkin. It is delicious on fresh, frozen or canned fruits, rice puddings, custards and adds a surprise to coffee or tea.

CLOVES: a dried flower bud of an East Indian tree. Cloves shine in dishes prepared with squash, sweet potatoes, fruit salad dressings, fruit compotes or medleys, applesauce, and baked items.

CORIANDER (AND CILANTRO): this is a European, South and Central American herb, similar to parsley. It can be used on almost all vegetables. It adds a characteristic scent and mild taste to soups and stews, is used in Mexican and Spanish dishes or as a garnish.

CUMIN: cumin is also a parsley-like relative. Its small white or rose-colored fruits are used primarily for pickling.

CURRY: curry is an East Indian spice combination, golden in color, rich in aroma, and handy in meat, fish, poultry and vegetable dishes. A delightful surprise is a light touch of curry added to fruit or fruit compotes. Some varieties contain hot peppers, so choose according to your own and your family's palate.

DILL SEED AND WEED: the bitter seed or dried, crushed leaves of another parsley-like plant. Dill is used as a pickling spice, enlivens lamb dishes, deviled eggs, a good combination spice used in breads. Complements certain vegetables such as peas, cabbage, carrots, cauliflower.

FENNEL: a tall herb with yellow flowers. The seeds are dried and used in cooking and flavoring. It has a licorice-like taste. Fennel is used in Italian dishes, pasta sauces, seafood dishes, and helps rid the palate of garlic taste and odor.

GARLIC: this is a small, bulblike plant. The bulb is made up of small sections, called cloves. It is strong smelling, and has a pungent taste and aroma. It adds body to salad dressings, meats, poultry, fish, sauces, gravies, vegetables and pasta dishes. Garlic is a remarkably universal spice, use sparingly.

GINGER: an Asiatic plant, whose ground-trailing root is dried, crushed and ground. Ginger livens fruits, fruit mixtures, cakes, puddings, dessert sauces. It is best with carrots, pumpkin, squash, apples, pears and grapefruit. Can be used sparingly in sauces, fish, poultry.

MARJORAM: a relative of the mint family, the leaves are dried and used whole or crushed for seasoning. It has a sweet, delicate flavor. Best used in shellfish dishes, veal and poultry dishes, cooked fruits, baked eggs and omelets.

MUSTARD: this is the dried, crushed and powdered seed of an annual plant. It has a bright yellow color, a strong scent and flavor. Mustard is a pungent seasoning for vegetable dishes and sauces, for fish, beef and ham. Use very sparingly.

NUTMEG: this is the hard seed of an East Indian plant. It is grated and dried to be used as a spice. The seed covering, also dried, crushed and powdered, is a spice known as mace. Both are used in fish and chicken dishes, cauliflower, broccoli and cabbage dishes. Nutmeg, a sweet spice, is also a delicate touch for baked goods, puddings, nut breads and dessert sauces.

ONION POWDER: this is dried, crushed and powdered onion bulb. Onion, akin to garlic, has a strong and characteristic flavoring and scent. It is used in all vegetable dishes, soups, sauces, stews, casseroles. It adds flavor to roast meats, poultry and legume dishes.

OREGANO: this is a cousin of the mint family. Oregano is used extensively in Italian cooking. It has sweet, pungent leaves which are dried and crushed or flaked. Good in vegetables, tomato and tomato sauces, soups and stews. A complementary herb for beef and chicken dishes.

PAPRIKA: paprika is the ground seed of certain chili pepper plants. It is mild, sometimes sweet and native to Europe and the United States. Paprika adds a marvelous, red-orange color as a garnish for salads, toppings on vegetables, poultry, or fish casseroles and on deviled eggs.

PARSLEY: this is a hollow-stemmed plant whose leaves are chopped and used fresh or dry. The best flavor is achieved by using fresh parsley. It is a colorful, bright green garnish, and can be used in almost any vegetable, fish, egg, poultry, cheese or meat dish.

PEPPER: this is the small dried fruit of an East Indian vine. Black pepper is the whole fruit, and white pepper is only the tender, inner portion of the fruit. It is used on salads, cheese, meat, poultry and fish dishes, in broths, soups and sauces. Use it with a light touch or it can be overpowering.

POPPY SEED: this is the small, dark seed of certain poppy plants. It is primarily used in baked goods, as a garnish for topping or breads and rolls.

ROSEMARY: this is a green plant of the mint family, native to the Mediterranean area of Europe. Its leaves are dried and crushed. It is used in Italian cuisine, and flavors soups, stews, sauces, vegetable dishes, poultry and fish.

SAGE: garden sage is a plant of the mint family—and the same as sagebrush. It adds zip to chicken and fish dishes, mild vegetables such as squash and eggplant, combines well with cheese and egg dishes and salad dressings.

TARRAGON: this is the leaves of the wormwood plant. It has a sweet flavor and aroma. It can be used in salad dressings, salads, sparingly in vegetable and poultry dishes.

THYME: this is also a mint family relative. Thyme is sweet and aromatic, best used in stews and brown sauces, tomato sauces, chicken, green beans, mushrooms, peas, omelets, egg dishes and aspics.

Herb Blends

FOR A SPECIAL SALAD BLEND:
    Mix: 4 parts each marjoram, basil, tarragon, parsley, celery
            seed and chives
            with
            1 part each thyme, and grated lemon peel

FOR A SAVORY VEGETABLE BLEND:
    Mix: 1 part each marjoram, basil, parsley and chives
            with
            ¼ part thyme

FOR A SUCCULENT EGG SEASONING BLEND:
    Mix: 3 parts parsley
            with
            1 part each tarragon, basil, marjoram and chives

FOR A SURPRISING ITALIAN BLEND:
    Mix: 2 parts each oregano, marjoram, thyme and basil
            with
            1 part each rosemary and sage

Gifts From Your Kitchen

Christmas? Birthdays? Anniversaries? What could be a better gift than something thoughtfully prepared in your own kitchen. It's a truly personal gift, and one that's good for the receiver, too.

Some attractive and tasty gift items can be:

Apple or strawberry butter, or chutney, packed in attractive airtight jars, sealed, wrapped or tied with a bow. Put a special label from your kitchen on these gifts, and you'll be in that person's mind whenever your gift is used.

Breakfast bars packed in a decorative tin...raspberry muffins tied into a pretty calico-print cloth and fastened with a ribbon...banana, pumpkin or applesauce bread wrapped in silver foil and topped with a colorful bow all have definite appeal.

Watch the grocery, drug and low-cost specialty stores for attractive bottles with corks or stoppers. Pack a special "secret" herb blend or salad dressing into one. Tie it up with a ribbon and your own special wishes for a happy celebration.

WEIGHTS AND MEASURES
1 teaspoon = 1/3 tablespoon
3 teaspoons = 1 tablespoon
1/8 cup = 2 tablespoons
1/4 cup = 4 tablespoons
1 cup = 1/2 pint
2 cups = 1 pint
2 pints = 1 quart
4 quarts = 1 gallon
1 pound = 16 ounces
1 fluid ounce = 2 tablespoons
16 fluid ounces = 1 pint

What The Doctor Ordered

We grow up amid the habits, customs and tastes of our families, our friends, and our environment. For the most part we in the 1980s are products of America in the past several decades. We have grown up with large quantities of salt and sugar, fast foods, prepared frozen/canned foods and, for most of us, a limited use of raw unprocessed products.

In the past 20 years there has been an explosion in the food industry. The public is more aware than ever of foods which are more sensible in relation to our well being. In response to this there is a wider variety and a greater quantity of fresh unadulterated foods available.

As one who has spent a good part of the past decade observing this greater culinary consumer, participating in cooking courses and food seminars and writing recipes and treating patients, I am excited by this wonderful book. The authors have combined their wide knowledge and experience into a volume which provides a basic understanding and then goes on to demonstrate with both recipes and menus. They have created exciting food ideas which combine the "new American cuisine" with other ethnic ideas of French, Greek, Oriental and Mexican, to mention but a few.

I think this book is going to be both instructional for you as well as fun to read and use.

Neil E. Romanoff, M.D., F.A.C.P.
Associate Director, Diabetes Education Program
Eisenhower Medical Center
Past President, Riverside County Heart Association

Suggested Menus

Recipes for most items presented within these sample menus are included on the following pages.

Breakfast

One Yeast Waffle
Strawberry Apple Butter 1-½ T.
Canadian Bacon 1 oz.

326 calories
16 grams protein
48 grams carbohy-
   drate
7 grams fat
85 mgs. cholesterol

505 mgs. sodium
4 grams dietary
   fiber
ADA Exchange Value
2 Starch/Bread
1 Lean Meat
1 Fruit
1 Fat

One Cornmeal Waffle
Strawberry Apple Butter 1-½ T.
One Egg

340 calories
15 grams protein
48 grams carbohy-
   drate
13 grams fat
271 mgs. cholesterol
254 mgs. sodium

3 grams dietary
   fiber
ADA Exchange Value
2 Starch/Bread
1 Medium-Fat Meat
1 Fruit
1 Fat

French Toast 2 slices
Raspberry Sauce 3 T.

304 calories
12 grams protein
42 grams carbohy-
   drate
8 grams fat
274 mgs. cholesterol

433 mgs. sodium
7 grams dietary
   fiber
ADA Exchange Value
2 Starch Bread
1 Medium-Fat Meat
1 Fruit
1 Fat

Cottage Cheese Pancakes 1 serving
  Strawberry Apple Butter 1½ T.

193	calories	298	mgs. sodium
13	grams protein	1	gram dietary fiber
23	grams carbohy-drate		ADA Exchange Value
		½	Starch/Bread
6	grams fat	1 ½	Medium-Fat Meat
71	mgs. cholesterol	1	Fruit

Brunch

Melon Balls ½ cup
Salmon Omelet Souffle 1 serving
One Raspberry Corn Muffin

350 calories	***ADA Exchange Value***
25 grams protein	*1 Starch/Bread*
36 grams carbohy-drate	*3 Lean Meat*
	½ Vegetable
11 grams fat	*1 Fruit*
212 cholesterol	*½ Fat*
573 mgs. sodium	
3 grams dietary fiber	

Strawberries 1¼ cups
Quiche 1 serving
One Whole Wheat Yeast Roll

322 calories	***ADA Exchange Value***
20 grams protein	*1 Starch/Bread*
42 grams carbohy-drate	*1 Lean Meat*
	1 Vegetable
9 grams fat	*1 Fruit*
165 mgs. cholesterol	*½ Nonfat Milk*
352 mgs. sodium	*1 Fat*
7 grams dietary fiber	

Blueberries ¾ cup
Italian Eggs 1 serving

349 calories	***ADA Exchange Value***
20 grams protein	*2 Starch/Bread*
49 grams carbohy-drate	*1 Lean Meat*
	1 Medium-Fat Meat
8 grams fat	*1 Vegetable*
229 mgs. cholesterol	*1 Fruit*
312 mgs. sodium	
5 grams dietary fiber	

Lunch

Chicken Salad 1 serving
Pita Bread 1 serving
Fresh Fruit Cup ½ cup

374 calories
30 grams protein
53 grams carbohy-
  drate
5 grams fat
73 mgs. cholesterol
75 mgs. sodium

7 grams dietary
  fiber
ADA Exchange Value
1½ Starch/Bread
3 Lean Meat
1 Vegetable
1½ Fruit

Ceviche 1 serving
Flour Tortillas 2
Blueberries ¾ cup

467 calories
30 grams protein
56 grams carbohy-
  drate
10 grams fat
25 mgs. cholesterol
143 mgs. sodium
10 grams dietary fi-
  ber

ADA Exchange Value
2 Starch/Bread
3 Lean Meat
3 Vegetable
1 Fruit
2 Fat

Pasta Salad 1 serving
Cantelope ⅓ melon

390 calories
25 grams protein
37 grams carbohy-
  drate
10 grams fat
48 mgs. cholesterol
81 mgs. sodium
6 grams dietary
  fiber

ADA Exchange Value
2 Starch/Bread
2 Lean Meat
1 Vegetable
1 Fruit
1 Fat

Rolled Taco 1 serving
Fresh Fruit Plate

540 calories
  49 grams protein
  63 grams carbohy-
    drate
  12 grams fat
106 mgs. cholesterol

750 mgs. sodium
  6 grams dietary
   fiber
ADA Exchange Value
  2 Starch/Bread
  5 Lean Meat
  2 Fruit

Dinner

Sherry Spinach Salad 1 serving
Stuffed Sole with Shrimp and Asparagus 1 serving
Parslied Potatos 1 serving
Glazed Carrots 1 serving
Fresh Fruit Plate with Dressing 1 serving

550 calories	**ADA Exchange Value**
45 grams protein	1 Starch/Bread
64 grams carbohydrate	5 Lean Meat
	2 ½ Vegetable
14 grams fat	2 Fruit
115 mgs. cholesterol	1 Fat
503 mgs. sodium	
10 grams dietary fiber	

Greek Salad 1 serving
Lamb Kebobs 1 serving
Ratatouille 1 serving
Bulgar Pilaf 1 serving
Apricot Pudding 1 serving

673 calories	**ADA Exchange Value**
37 grams protein	1 ½ Starch/Bread
76 grams carbohydrate	2 ½ Lean Meat
	4 Vegetable
15 grams fat	1 Fruit
69 mgs. cholesterol	4 Fat
361 mgs. sodium	
13 grams dietary fiber	

Dinner (con't)

Bib Lettuce Salad with Radishes 1 serving
Vinaigrette Dressing
½ Cornish Game Hen with Orange Sauce
Roasted Potatos 1 serving
Stuffed Tomato with Peas 1 serving
Chocolate Souffle 1 serving

611 calories	***ADA Exchange Value***
42 grams protein	*3 Starch/Bread*
76 grams carbohy-	*3 Lean Meat*
drate	*2 Vegetable*
15 grams fat	*1 Fruit*
90 mgs. cholesterol	*½ Nonfat Milk*
647 mgs. sodium	*2 Fat*
9 grams dietary	
fiber	

Caesar Salad 1 serving
Flank Steak Roulade 1 serving
Spinach and Water Chestnut Stuffing
Potato Pie 1 serving
Mushrooms and Chinese Peas 1 serving
Brown Rice Pudding 1 serving

623 calories	***ADA Exchange Value***
47 grams protein	*3 Starch/Bread*
82 grams carbohy-	*3 Lean Meat*
drate	*4 Vegetable*
12 grams fat	*1 Fruit*
41 mgs. cholesterol	*1 Fat*
1073 mgs. sodium	
13 grams dietary	
fiber	

Dinner (con't)

Spinach Salad with Strawberries I serving
Poppy Seed Dressing
Chicken Breast Supreme I serving
"Wild" Brown Rice I serving
Panned Green Beans I serving
Lemon Cheese Pie I serving

643 calories	*ADA Exchange Value*
49 grams protein	2½ Starch/Bread
48 grams carbohy-drate	4 Lean Meat
	1 Medium-Fat Meat
29 grams fat	2 Vegetable
99 mgs. cholesterol	3 Fat
1093 mgs. sodium	
6 grams dietary fiber	

Waldorf Salad I serving
BBQ Chicken Breasts I serving
Herbed Stuffed Potatos I serving
Julienne Carrots and Zucchini I serving
Upside Down Apple Gingerbread I serving

638 calories	*ADA Exchange Value*
37 grams protein	2½ Starch/Bread
75 grams carbohy-drate	4 Lean Meat
	2 Vegetable
22 grams fat	1½ Fruit
87 mgs. cholesterol	3½ Fat
549 mgs. sodium	
8 grams dietary fiber	

Breakfast, Brunch & Lunch

BREAKFAST MAKES CHAMPIONS . . .

"*I* have no time for breakfast!" This seems to be a common cry of many who, by choice or necessity, live in today's fast lane. Ironically, if your first decision for the day is to skip breakfast, you'll be getting off to a poor start—which certainly needn't be the case ...the problem is easily solved with a *minimum* of preparation and effort. This chapter contains recipes for breads, muffins, waffles, pancakes and breakfast bars which can be made ahead in batches, individually wrapped and frozen. Then, each is readily available. They can be removed from the freezer a few at a time, popped into the oven or toaster for a quick and nutritious breakfast, snack, afternoon gettogether, luncheon accompaniment—and so on.

Build a reputation as a well-prepared hostess, with a sturdy supply of these tasty and good-for-you items tucked into your freezer for unexpected drop-in guests, an unscheduled visit of the hungry team after practice. And take them along when *you're* invited as a dinner guest. Delight your hostess with a homemade and handy treat.

Remember, too, most of these recipes are portable...so they can be toted to work for desk-top breakfast, lunch or snack. When the kids come in hungry from school, play or practice, these items are guiltless galore—high in nutritional value, easy to prepare and have on hand.

Rediscover breakfast! Do away with those midmorning lows! And celebrate the joy of cooking!

Banana Bran Muffins
A high fiber treat

1 cup whole wheat flour	3 teaspoons baking powder
½ cup uncooked oatmeal (not instant)	3 tablespoons dark molasses
1 cup unprocessed bran	2 very ripe bananas mashed
1 whole egg	1 cup nonfat milk
⅔ cup raisins	

1. Preheat oven to 400 degrees.

2. Combine all dry ingredients.

3. Add rest of ingredients except raisins, mix well.

4. Fold in raisins.

5. Spoon batter into 12 muffin tins sprayed with a nonstick spray or lined with paper baking cups.

6. Bake 15-20 minutes.

Makes 12 muffins.

Each Muffin Contains:

138 calories	107 mgs. sodium
5 grams protein	3 grams dietary fiber
28 grams carbohydrate	
1 gram fat	**ADA Exchange Value**
23 mgs. cholesterol	2 Starch/Bread

Bran Muffins

1 cup unprocessed bran
1 cup whole wheat flour
1 tablespoon fructose
1½ teaspoons baking soda

1 egg
2 egg whites
1 cup buttermilk
¼ cup corn oil
2 tablespoons honey
¼ cup molasses

1. Preheat oven to 350 degrees.

2. Combine bran, flour, fructose and baking soda in a bowl.

3. Mix together egg, egg whites, buttermilk, corn oil, honey and molasses.

4. Stir liquid mixture into flour mixture, stir to moisten.

5. Pour batter into 12 paper lined muffins tins. (Or spray muffins tins with non-stick spray.)

6. Bake for 25 minutes. Cool.

Makes 12 muffins.

Each Muffin Contains:

143 calories
4 grams protein
19 grams carbohydrate
6 grams fat
24 mgs. cholesterol

146 mgs. sodium
2 grams dietary fiber

ADA Exchange Value
1 Starch/Bread
1 Fat

Oatmeal Breakfast Bars

Delicious for a breakfast on the go, to carry for snacks or even for a dessert.

⅓ cup corn oil margarine
½ cup fructose
6 egg whites
½ cup nonfat milk
2 tablespoons molasses
2½ teaspoons vanilla
1 pk. dry Butter Buds
1 cup whole wheat flour
1 cup unprocessed bran
3 cup rolled oats, uncooked
1 teaspoon baking powder
2 teaspoons cinnamon
1 cup raisins

1. Preheat oven to 350 degrees.

2. Cream together margarine and fructose.

3. Add eggs whites, milk, molasses, vanilla, and Butter Buds and mix well.

4. Stir in flour, baking powder, bran, oats, cinnamon, raisins and mix.

5. Put mixture in a 9x13 inch pan that has been sprayed with a nonstick spray.

6. Bake 15 minutes. Cool, cut into 16 bars.

Each bar contains:

206 calories
7 grams protein
34 grams carbohydrate
5 grams fat
0 mgs cholesterol
90 mgs. sodium

3 grams dietary fiber

ADA Exchange Value
2 Starch/Bread
1 Fat

Raspberry Corn Muffins

These are tasty muffins with a surprise inside. They freeze well and are good for breakfast or as an accompaniment to a salad.

I cup cornmeal	2 tablespoons corn oil
I cup whole wheat pastry flour	I tablespoon fructose
I tablespoon baking powder	36 raspberries (approx. ¾ cup)
I cup nonfat milk	
2 egg whites	

1. Preheat oven to 400 degrees.

2. Combine cornmeal, flour and baking powder in a large mixing bowl.

3. Combine milk, egg whites, corn oil, fructose, and mix well.

4. Add liquid ingredients to dry and mix well.

5. Spray 12 muffin tins, with a nonstick spray or line with paper cups. Fill each to ¼ full.

6. Place 3 raspberries in the center of each, top with rest of batter.

7. Bake 20 minutes or until golden brown.

Makes 12 muffins.

Each muffin contains:

109 calories	**ADA Exchange Value**
3 grams protein	**I Starch/Bread**
17 grams carbohydrate	**½ Fat**
3 grams fat	
0 mgs. cholesterol	
104 mgs. sodium	
.7 grams dietary fiber	

Carrot, Prune Muffin

⅓ cup fructose
¼ cup light molasses
2 eggs
1 cup grated carrots
1 cup pitted and chopped prunes
½ cup nonfat milk
1 cup oatmeal (grind into flour in food processor or blender)
½ cup unprocessed bran
1 cup whole wheat flour

2 teaspoons baking powder
1 teaspoon ground cinnamon
½ teaspoon nutmeg
¼ teaspoon ground ginger
¼ teaspoon ground cloves
¼ teaspoon baking soda
½ cup chopped walnuts

1. Preheat oven to 350 degrees.

2. Mix fructose, molasses, eggs, carrots, prunes, and milk together.

3. Mix all dry ingredients, except nuts. Add ½ to wet ingredients mix lightly. Add the rest of the dry ingredients, mix, add nuts last.

4. Spray 12 muffins tins with nonstick coating and fill.

5. Bake 25 minutes, let stand 15 minutes before removing from pan.

Makes 12 muffins.

Each muffin contains:

196 calories
6 grams protein
34 grams carbohydrate
5 grams fat
46 mgs. cholesterol

96 mgs. sodium
3 grams dietary fiber

ADA Exchange Value
2 Starch/Bread
1 Fat

Apple Walnuts Muffins

¾ cup unbleached flour

¾ cup wholewheat flour

½ cup unprocessed bran

2½ teaspoons baking powder

1 teaspoon cinnamon

¼ teaspoon nutmeg

2 eggs

⅔ cup concentrated apple juice

1 large apple cored and chopped

½ cup walnuts

1. Preheat oven to 400 degrees.

2. Mix all dry ingredients in food processor or blender until well mixed together.

3. Mix eggs, apple juice, apple and walnuts together.

4. Pour liquid ingredients into dry ingredients and mix until well moistened.

5. Fill 12 nonstick muffins tins that have been sprayed with a non-stick spray or lined with paper cups.

6. Bake 20 minutes.

Makes 12 muffins.

Each muffin contains:

141 calories

4 grams protein

22 grams carbohydrate

5 grams fat

46 mgs. cholesterol

185 mgs. sodium

2 grams dietary fiber

ADA Exchange Value

1 ½ **Starch/Bread**

1 **Fat**

Cottage Cheese Pancakes

These pancakes have a soft, delicate texture and are delicious served with fresh fruit or apple butter.
(page 135)

I cup low fat cottage cheese
I whole egg
4 egg whites

¼ cup whole wheat flour
I tablespoon corn oil

1. Process cottage cheese in blender or food processor until smooth.

2. Add egg, egg whites and blend.

3. Add flour and oil, blend just until mixed.

4. Use ¼ cup measure for each pancake, bake pancakes on hot griddle (sprayed with nonstick spray) until they bubble, turn and bake until firm and browned.

Makes 8 pancakes, I serving = 2 pancakes

Each serving contains:

132 calories
13 grams protein
7 grams carbohydrate
6 grams fat
71 mgs. cholesterol

297 mgs.. sodium
.1 gram dietary fiber

ADA Exchange Value
½ **Starch/Bread**
1 ½ **Medium - Fat Meat**

Yeast Waffles

The beauty of these is that you can make up the whole batch and freeze what's left over. Just pop them in a toaster for a quick breakfast during the week or for a snack. They are good and crunchy just by themselves.

1 package dry yeast
2 cups lukewarm nonfat milk (105 to 115 degrees)
2 egg yolks
1 teaspoon vanilla
1 cup sifted whole wheat pastry flour
1½ cups sifted unbleached flour

1 tablespoon fructose
2 tablespoons corn oil margarine, melted
2 teaspoons dry Butter Buds
4 egg whites

1. Sprinkle yeast over warm milk, stir to dissolve.

2. Beat egg yolks and vanilla add to milk.

3. Sift flour and fructose, add to milk mixture.

4. Stir in melted margarine and Butter Buds, combine thoroughly.

5. Beat egg whites until stiff, fold into batter.

6. Let mixture stand in warm place for 45 minutes or until double in bulk.

7. Use ½ cup per waffle and bake according to direction for your waffle iron.

Makes 8 waffles.

Each waffle contains:

213 calories
9 grams protein
32 grams carbohydrate
5 grams fat
69 mgs. cholesterol
66 mgs.. sodium

2.5 grams dietary fiber

ADA Exchange Value
2 Starch/Bread
1 Fat

Cornmeal Waffles

These waffles have marvelous, crunchy texture and are especially good with Strawberry Apple Butter (page 135). Freeze leftovers and toast.

½ cup whole wheat flour
1 cup cornmeal
2-½ teaspoons baking powder
1 tablespoon fructose
2 teaspoons dry Butter Buds

¼ cup unprocessed bran
1 tablespoon corn oil margarine, melted
2 cups nonfat milk
2 egg whites, beaten until stiff

1. Sift flour, cornmeal, baking powder, fructose, and Butter Buds into a mixing bowl.

2. Add bran and mix.

3. Add melted margarine and milk, mix well.

4. Fold in beaten egg whites.

5. Bake in preheated waffle iron according to directions for your waffle iron, best when very brown and crisp.

Makes 6 waffles.

Each waffle contains:

199 calories
8 grams protein
32 grams carbohydrate
5 grams fat
1 mgs.. cholesterol
2.5 mgs. sodium

1.6 grams dietary fiber

ADA Exchange Value
2 Starch/Bread
1 Fat

French Toast

This is easy and fast to make for one person, just divide by four. Serve with Raspberry Sauce or Strawberry Apple Butter (page 134, 135).

4 whole eggs
¼ cup non fat milk
1 teaspoon vanilla
¼ teaspoon nutmeg

1 teaspoon cinnamon
8 slices whole wheat bread

1. Mix all ingredients, except bread, together in a flat bowl that will hold one slice of bread.

2. Dip each piece of bread in egg mixture, making sure all is soaked up.

3. Brown bread in large skillet sprayed with nonstick coating. (if your skillet will not hold 2 slices of bread, cut slices in half so it can fit more).

Makes 4 servings. 1 serving = 2 slices French Toast

Each serving contains:

224 calories
12 grams protein
27 grams carbohy-
    drate
8 grams fat
274 mgs.. cholesterol
433 mgs.. sodium

6 grams dietary
fiber

ADA Exchange Value
2 Starch/Bread
1 Medium - Fat Protein
1 Fat

Italian Eggs

¾ cup chicken broth
2 cups mushrooms, sliced
1 medium onion, sliced
1 bell pepper, sliced
½ teaspoon Italian Blend (page 22) dash of crushed hot red pepper

4 red potatoes, cooked and sliced in large pieces
3 whole eggs
3 egg whites

1. Reduce ½ cup broth to 1 tablespoon in a nonstick skillet.

2. Saute mushrooms and set aside.

3. Reduce ¼ cup broth to 1 tablespoon and saute onion and bell pepper until tender.

4. Add seasonings, potato, and mushrooms, toss until warm.

5. Beat eggs and egg whites together, add to vegetables stirring until set.

Makes 4 servings.

Each serving contains:

289 calories
20 grams protein
34 grams carbohydrate
8 grams fat
229 mgs.. cholesterol
311 mgs.. sodium

3 grams dietary fiber

ADA Exchange Value
2 Starch/Bread
1 Lean Protein
1 Medium - Fat Protein
1 Vegetable

Quiche

This can be a very versatile dish. You can use any leftover vegetables, be creative and have fun!

1/4 cup chicken broth
1/2 teaspoon garlic, minced
2 medium zucchini, shredded and well drained
2 tablespoons parmesan cheese, grated
1/2 lb. broccoli, chopped and steamed
1-1/4 cups nonfat milk + 3 tablespoons nonfat dry milk powder

3 ounces low-fat cheese shredded
2 eggs, separated
1 egg white
2 tablespoons tomato paste
1 tablespoon dried basil leaves, crushed
dash red pepper

1. Preheat oven to 350 degrees.

2. Reduce chicken broth in a nonstick skillet to 1 tablespoon. Add minced garlic and saute 1 minute, add shredded zucchini and cook about 3 minutes, add 1 tablespoon parmesan cheese and cook 1 more minute.

3. Spray the bottom of an 8" quiche pan with a nonstick. Spread vegetable mixture thinly on the bottom of the pan to form a crust.

4. Arrange broccoli on top, sprinkle with shredded lowfat cheese.

5. Mix nonfat milk, nonfat milk powder and egg yolks.

6. Add tomato paste, basil leaves and red pepper.

7. Beat egg whites until stiff and fold into milk mixture.

8. Pour mixture into quiche pan and sprinkle with 1 tablespoon of parmesan cheese.

9. Bake for 30 minutes or until set in center.

Makes 4 servings.

Each serving contains:

184 calories
17 grams protein
13 grams carbohy-
drate
8 grams fat
153 mgs.. cholesterol
332 mgs.. sodium

2.5 grams dietary
fiber

ADA Exchange Value
1 Lean Meat
1 Vegetable
½ Nonfat Milk
1 Fat

Salmon Omelet Souffle

This is a quick and tasty dish that is also good served cold.

1 7 ¾ ounce can of salmon	¼ cup green onion chopped
2 eggs	⅛ teaspoon dill weed
2 egg whites	
2 tablespoons tomato paste	

1. Preheat oven to 350 degrees.

2. Beat eggs until frothy, fold in the rest of ingredients.

3. Pour in 9" baking dish that has been sprayed with nonstick spray.

4. Bake for 20 minutes or until done.

Makes 3 servings.

Each serving contains:

181 calories
22 grams protein
4 grams carbohydrate
8 grams fat
212 mgs.. cholesterol
468 mgs.. sodium

.3 grams dietary fiber

ADA Exchange Value
3 Lean Meat
½ Vegetable

Ceviche

A colorful and different dish, it's great drained and stuffed into a pita pocket with lettuce or on a warmed tortilla.

1 pound fresh white fish, diced
1/4 cup lime juice
1/4 cup lemon juice
1 tablespoon olive oil
1 tablespoon cilantro, fresh or dried
2 cloves garlic, pressed
1 jalapeno pepper, peeled, seeded and chopped
1/2 teaspoon sweet basil
1/2 teaspoon fresh ground black pepper
1/2 cup celery, chopped
1 medium red onion chopped
2 medium tomatoes, chopped with juice and seeds
1 medium green or red sweet pepper, diced
1 medium cucumber, peeled and chopped

1. Combine lemon juice, lime juice, oil, cilantro, garlic, jalapeno pepper, basil and black pepper in a blender and chop.

2. Put chopped vegetables and diced fish in a bowl.

3. Pour lemon juice mixture over vegetables and fish and toss.

4. Cover tightly and refrigerate 24 hours. The acid in the juice "cooks" the fish. Everything is spicy, but mild with no fish taste.

Makes 4 servings.

Each serving contains:

263 calories
24 grams protein
13 grams carbohydrate
8 grams fat
25 mgs.. cholesterol
109 mgs.. sodium

3.3 grams dietary fiber

ADA Exchange Value
3 Lean Meat
3 Vegetable

Tuna Salad

This lo-cal version of its traditional cousin is yummy on rolls, stuffed into pita pockets or served on a bed of lettuce and garnished with crisp, raw vegetables.

1 7 ½ ounce can tuna, water-packed
1 stalk celery, finely chopped

1 green onion, finely chopped
pepper to taste
¼ cup low calorie mayonnaise

1. Combine ingredients and chill.

Makes 3 servings.

Each serving contains:

138 calories
19 grams protein
3 grams carbohydrate
6 grams fat
49 mgs.. cholesterol
243 mgs.. sodium

.5 grams dietary fiber

ADA Exchange Value
2 Lean Meat
½ Vegetable

Chicken or Turkey Salad

Try a Raspberry Corn Muffin (page 40) or toasted English muffin with Strawberry-Apple Butter (page 135) on the side for a festive luncheon.

12 ounces turkey or chicken breast with skin removed, steamed or baked and diced

3 stalks celery, diced

¼ cup raisins

2 teaspoons sesame seeds

½ teaspoon celery seed

1 tablespoon sour cream

1 tablespoon low calorie mayonnaise

1 large apple, diced

1. Combine all ingredients. Mix well and chill.

2. Serve on lettuce leaves garnished with carrot sticks or curls.

Makes 4 servings.

Each serving contains:

194 calories
26 grams protein
14 grams carbohydrate
3 grams fat
73 mgs.. cholesterol
74 mgs.. sodium

2 grams dietary fiber

ADA Exchange Value
3 Lean Meat
1 Vegetable
½ Fruit

Rolled Tacos

When you're in the mood for Mexican food, these are fun, easy and satisfy the urge!

2 pounds chicken breasts, boned, skinned, and split
2 cups green chili salsa

1 dozen corn tortillas
shredded lettuce

1. Preheat oven to 300 degrees.
2. Rinse chicken breasts and place in a casserole.
3. Pour salsa over chicken, cover and bake 1½ hours. Cool.
4. Shred chicken and put back in sauce. Reheat when ready to use.
5. Place 1/12 mixture in 1 warmed corn tortilla and roll it up.
6. Serve on a bed of shredded lettuce.

1 serving = 2 rolled tacos.

Makes 6 servings.
Each Serving Contains:

360 calories
41 grams protein
33 grams carbohydrate
8 grams fat

96 mgs. cholesterol
494 mgs.. sodium
3 grams dietary fiber

ADA Exchange Value
2 Starch/Bread
4 Lean Meat

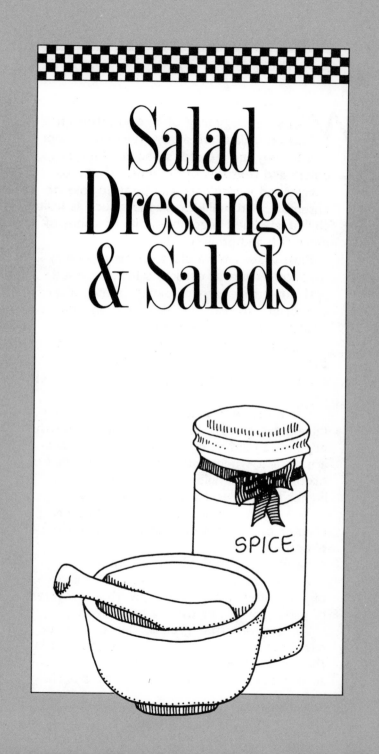

Salad Dressings & Salads

SPICE

A NOTE ON SALADS

What's the beginning of a good salad? Imagination! Salads are an eye-pleaser, an appetite tickler, and a dieter's delight. All types, colors and textures of "greens," the traditional salad ingredients, can be used solo or ensemble, with unlikley partners such as fruits, chilled, steamed vegetables, bits or cubes of meat, fish and poultry.

Plus, salads have a place for almost every situation. A hearty chicken salad, garnished with tomatoes, carrots, pimento, etc., makes a colorful, satisfying and delicious luncheon, a brunch selection, or sandwich filling.

Vegetable salads don't *have* to be served *before* a meal. In fact, in many European countries the salad concludes the meal to help aid digestion.

For those with a little to lose, a fresh vegetable salad is filling, bright, lively and takes the edge off a hungry, growling stomach. Salads are perfect when watching calories. Instead of taking a second helping of something much higher in calories, fill up on your salad.

The salads and dressings included in this chapter offer variety and low-calorie high nutrition.

Salad preparation begins by washing "greens" carefully in cold water. Dry thoroughly, either by patting dry with a few layers of paper towels, or using a spin dryer.

After drying the "greens," put in a plastic bag, press out the air, tie the bag and chill in the refrigerator until ready to serve. This ensures fresh color, taste and a crispy crunch.

A timesaver, when making a vegetable salad that's full of lots of different ingredients, clean, peel, cut, dice and chop extra. You can store these in the refrigerator in covered airtight containers and have a ready-made salad handy. Fresh vegetables, cleaned and prepared for salad ingredients will store nicely without losing color or taste for four or five days.

Fruit Salad Dressing

1½ cup low fat cottage cheese
¼ cup nonfat yogurt
¼ cup sour cream
2 teaspoons fresh orange juice

½ teaspoon fresh orange rind, grated
¼ teaspoon vanilla
1 teaspoon honey

1. Combine all ingedients in a blender or food processor and blend until smooth.

2. Chill and serve over fresh, canned or frozen and thawed fruit.

Makes 4 servings.

Each serving contains:

92 calories
7 grams protein
7 grams carbohydrate
4 grams fat
10 mgs.. cholesterol

165 mgs.. sodium
0 grams dietary fiber

ADA Exchange Value
1 Medium - Fat Protein
½ Fruit

Poppy Seed Dressing
for Spinach Salad with Strawberries

1 egg white
1 packet Equal, or
    1/2 tablespoon
    fructose
1 1/2 teaspoons dijon
    style mustard
1/4 cup raspberry
    vinegar (or apple
    cider vinegar)

1/4 cup water
1/2 cup corn oil
1 tablespoon poppy
    seeds

1. Combine egg white, Equal, mustard, vinegar, and water in blender.

2. While blender is running, slowly drizzle in corn oil, blend until well mixed.

3. Pour into storage container and add 1 tablespoon poppy seeds.

4. Makes 1 cup.

1 serving = 2 tablespoons
Each Serving Contains:

129 calories
1 gram protein
1 gram carbohy-
    drate
14 grams fat
0 mgs.. cholesterol

19 mgs.. sodium
0 grams dietary
    fiber
ADA Exchange Value
3 Fats

Sherry Dressing

1 ½ teaspoons olive oil

3 tablespoons wine vinegar

3 tablespoons dry sherry

3 tablespoons water

½ teaspoon fresh ground black pepper

1. Combine all ingredients in a blender or covered container and mix well.

2. Chill

3. Makes ¾ cup.

1 serving = 2 tablespoons

Each Serving Contains:

18 calories

0 gram protein

1 gram carbohydrate

1 gram fat

0 mgs.. cholesterol

1 mg. sodium

0 grams dietary fiber

ADA Exchange Value calories negligible per serving

Greek Salad Dressing

Also an excellent marinade for beef, lamb, or chicken.

2 tablespoons olive oil

3 garlic cloves, minced

¼ cup lemon juice

½ teaspoon cilantro (coriander)

2 teaspoons oregano

⅔ cup white wine vinegar

dash of cayenne pepper

1. Combine all ingredient in a blender or covered container and blend well.

2. Store in a covered container and chill.

3. Makes I cup.

I serving = 2 tablespoons

Each serving contains:

37 calories

0 grams protein

2 grams carbohydrate

3 grams fat

0 mgs. cholesterol

I mg. sodium

0 grams dietary fiber

ADA Exchange Value

I Fat

Vinaigrette Dressing

1/4 cup olive oil
1/2 teaspoon garlic powder
2 teaspoons Worcestershire Sauce
1 teaspoon dry mustard
dash Tabasco sauce

1/2 teaspoon ground black pepper
juice from 1/2 lemon
1 cup wine vinegar (red or white)
1 cup water

1. Combine all ingredients in a blender or covered container and mix well.

2. Store in a covered container. Chill.

3. Makes 2 cups.

1 serving = 2 tablespoons

Each Serving Contains:

33 calories
0 grams protein
1 gram carbohydrate
3 grams fat
0 mgs.. cholesterol

6 mgs.. sodium
0 grams dietary fiber
ADA Exchange Value
1 Fat

Variations of Vinaigrette
used in other recipes

Caesar Dressing

½ cup Vinaigrette
   dressing
1 egg

2 tablespoons
   parmesan cheese,
   grated

1. Combine ingredients and chill.

Makes 4 servings.

Each Serving Contains:

48 calories
3 grams protein
2 grams carbohy-
   drate
4 grams fat

71 mgs.. cholesterol
82 mgs.. sodium
0 grams dietary
   fiber
ADA Exchange Value
1 Fat

Basil Dressing

½ **Vinaigrette dressing**

½ **teaspoon basil (crushed with mortar and pestle)**

1. Combine ingredients and chill.

Makes 4 servings.

Each Serving Contains:

- **33 calories**
- **0 grams protein**
- **1 gram carbohy-drate**
- **0 mgs.. cholesterol**
- **6 mgs.. sodium**
- **0 grams dietary fiber**
- **ADA Exchange Value**
- **1 Fat**

Sherry Spinach Salad

2 bunches fresh spinach
¼ red onion, sliced very thin

1 hard boiled egg, finely chopped
½ cup Sherry Dressing (page 59)

1. Wash spinach carefully, as each leaf can hold dirt.

2. Break the stems off the leaves, drain, spin or pat dry.

3. Put in a bowl with onions and toss with dressing.

4. Place on four salad plates and sprinkle each with ¼ chopped egg.

5. Makes 4 servings.

Each serving contains:

54 calories
4 grams protein
4 grams carbohydrate
3 grams fat

68 mgs.. cholesterol
84 mgs.. sodium
3 grams dietary fiber
ADA Exchange Value
1 Vegetable
1 Fat

Greek Salad

1 green pepper, sliced

2 large tomatoes, cut in wedges

1 cucumber, cut in half lengthwise, scoop out seeds and slice

1 small red onion, thinly sliced

1 cup Greek Dressing (page 60)

½ cup Farmers cheese, broken into small pieces**

1. Toss pepper, tomatoes, cucumber and onion in a bowl.

2. Pour Greek Dressing over vegetables and let marinate in refrigerator 2 to 3 hours.

3. Add cheese just before serving.

Makes 4 servings.

Each Serving Contains:

189 calories
9 grams protein
14 grams carbohydrate
12 grams fat
16 mgs.. cholesterol
48 mgs.. sodium

3 grams dietary fiber

ADA Exchange Value
½ Lean Meat
3 Vegetable
2 Fat

**See Hints about Ingredients, page , for cheese substitutions.

Caesar Salad

1 large head
  romaine lettuce
½ cup Caesar Salad
  Dressing (page 62)
1 cup Crunchy
  Croutons
  (page 137)

2 tablespoons par-
  mesan cheese,
  freshly grated

1. Wash romaine lettuce well, drain and tear into bite-sized pieces, spin or pat dry.

2. Add dressing and toss well.

3. Add croutons and toss lightly.

4. Place on 4 salad plates and sprinkle each with ½ tablespoon parmesan cheese.

Makes 4 servings.

Each serving contains:

92 calories
 4 grams protein
 8 grams carbohy-
   drate
 5 grams fat
20 mgs.. cholesterol

166 mgs.. sodium
  2 grams dietary
    fiber
ADA Exchange Value
  1 Vegetable
  1 Fat

Bib Lettuce With Radishes

2 heads bib lettuce
1 bunch of radishes,
thinly sliced

½ cup Vinaigrette
Dressing (page 61)

1. Wash bib lettuce, drain and tear into bit-sized pieces, spin or pat dry.

2. Toss lettuce, radishes, and dressing together and place on four salad plates.

Makes 4 servings.

Each serving contains:

53 calories
1 gram protein
5 grams carbohy-
drate
4 grams fat
0 mgs.. cholesterol

21 mgs.. sodium
2 grams dietary
fiber
ADA Exchange Value
1 Vegetable
1 Fat

Antipasto Salad

9 ounce package
frozen artichoke
hearts (steam 2
minutes)
2 cups green beans,
cut into 3 inch
pieces (steam 5
minutes)
1 green or red
sweet pepper,
sliced (steam 2
minutes)

1 cucumber, cut in
half lengthwise,
seed and slice
1/4 pound fresh mush-
rooms sliced
1/2 cup Greek Salad
Dressing (page 60)

1. Toss all ingredients, cover and chill for several hours, stirring
occasionally.

Makes 4 generous servings.

Each serving contains:

104 calories
4 grams protein
17 grams carbohy-
drate
4 grams fat
0 mgs.. cholesterol

20 mgs.. sodium
4 grams dietary
fiber
ADA Exchange Value
3 Vegetables
1 Fat

Spinach Salad With Strawberries

2 bunches fresh
spinach

½ cup Poppy Seed
Dressing (page 58)

12 strawberries cut
in half

1. Wash spinach carefully as each can hold dirt, break the stems off leaves, spin or pat dry.

2. Toss spinach with dressing.

3. Place on four serving plates and garnish each with 6 strawberry halves.

Makes 4 servings.

Each serving contains:

159 calories
3 grams protein
7 grams carbohy-
drate
15 grams fat
0 mgs.. cholesterol

86 mgs.. sodium
3 grams dietary
fiber
ADA Exchange Value
1 Vegetable
3 Fat

Tomato Cucumber Salad

1 cucumber, peeled and sliced	½ cup Basil Dressing (page 63)
1 large tomato, sliced	
4 romaine leaves washed and patted dry	

1. Marinate cucumber and tomato in Basil Dressing 2 hours

2. On 4 salad plates place 1 romaine leaf each and ¼ of marinated cucumbers and tomatoes.

Makes 4 servings.

Each serving contains:

60 calories	12 mgs.. sodium
1 grams protein	2 grams dietary fiber
6 grams carbohy-drate	**ADA Exchange Value**
4 grams fat	1 Vegetable
0 mgs.. cholesterol	1 Fat

Waldorf Salad

2 small apples,
cored and
chopped
2 stalks celery,
chopped
1/4 cup raisins
8 walnut halves,
chopped

1/4 cup sour cream
2 tablespoons
low-calorie
mayonnaise
1/8 teaspoon nutmeg

1. Combine apples, celery, raisins and walnuts.

2. Mix sour cream with low calorie mayonnaise and nutmeg.

3. Add sour cream mixture to apple mixture.

4. Cover and chill.

Makes 4 servings.

Each Serving Contains:

170 calories
2 grams protein
21 grams carbohy-
drate
10 grams fat
9 mgs.. cholesterol
28 mgs.. sodium

3 grams dietary
fiber
ADA Exchange Value
1 Vegetable
1 Fruit
2 Fat

Hint, to keep apples from turning brown toss them in 2 cups cold water with the juice of 1/2 of a lemon, pat dry on paper towels.

Pasta Salad

3 cups cooked pasta
shells

2 stalks celery,
sliced

2 green onions or
scallions, sliced

2 cups broccoli flo-
werettes, steamed
crisp tender (3-5
minutes)

8 ounces cooked
and cubed chick-
en, turkey, or wa-
ter packed tuna

1 cup Vinaigrette
Dressing (page 61)

½ teaspoon crushed
basil (optional)

1. Combine all ingredients and chill 2-3 hours.

2. Serve on a bed of lettuce.

Makes 4 servings.

Each serving contains:

330 calories
25 grams protein
37 grams carbohy-
drate
10 grams fat
48 mgs.. cholesterol
81 mgs.. sodium

4 grams dietary
fiber

ADA Exchange Value
2 Starch/Bread
2 Lean Meat
1 Vegetable
1 Fat

Vegetables

NATURE'S BOUNTY

Vegetables are truly nature's bounty. Each season and time of year, an abundance of tastes, textures and hues of vegetables attract our eye. Vegetables make wonderful combinations, add a zippy, color-spot on a luncheon, dinner or salad plate. Most vegetables are also high in fiber, contain protein, vitamins and minerals—so they are honest-to-goodness *good food,* too. For maximum flavor, color and texture retention, we recommend serving vegetables raw, lightly sauteed in broth or stock, steamed or quickly stir-fried in a little oil. The longer the cooking time, the less flavor is retained, the mushier the texture and the lower the natural vitamin and mineral content.

Vegetable sparklers can include simple toppings, such as crushed cereals, croutons, grated cheeses, herbs and spices. Vegetables can be combined with meats, fish and poultry and baked into a casserole dish, added to cubed or diced meats and poulty and served over rice, noodles or bulgar for a quick, easy and fortifying main dish meal.

Try leaving all or part of the salt out, and experimenting with herbs and spices on your vegetables. The true, delicate or bold flavor of the vegetable will shine, and will have your family asking for *more*!

SUPER LOW-CALORIE VEGETABLES INCLUDE:

Chicory

Chinese Cabbage

Cucumbers

Endive

Escarole

Lettuce

Parsley

Radishes

and

Watercress

MODERATELY LOW-CALORIE VEGETABLES INCLUDE:

Artichoke

Asparagus

Bean Sprouts

Beets

Broccoli

Brussels Sprouts

Cabbage

Carrots

Cauliflower

Celery

Eggplant

Green Pepper

Greens

Beet

Chard

Chollard

Greens (cont.)

Dandelion

Kale

Mustard

Spinach

Turnip

Mushrooms

Okra

Onions

Rhubarb

Rutabaga

String Beans

Summer Squash

Tomatoes

Turnips

Zucchini

STARCHY, OR MODERATELY HIGH-CALORIE VEGETABLES INCLUDE:

Corn

Corn on the Cob

Lima Beans

Parsnips

Green Peas

White Potatoes

Mashed Potatoes

Pumpkin

Winter Squash, Acorn or

Butternut

Yam or Sweet Potato

Dried peas, lentils and beans, although also known as "legumes," are in the starchy vegetable category.

Steaming Chart

VEGETABLE	MINUTES
Artichokes	45
Asparagus	15
Beets, quartered	15
Broccoli	3-5
Brussels Sprouts	5
Cabbage, quartered	5
Carrots, ½-in. sliced	5
Cauliflower	3-5
Corn	3
Eggplant, cut or sliced	5
Green Beans	5
Mushrooms	2
Peas	3-5
Peas, snow	2
Peppers, green and red	2
Potatoes	
Sweet ½-in. sliced	15
White ½-in. sliced	10
Spinach	1-2
Squash	
Acorn or Hubbard	5
Summer or Zucchini	3

Tasty Brussles Sprouts

1 pound fresh Brus-
sels sprouts
washed and
trimmed (or 2
packages frozen,
thawed)

½ cup chicken broth
1 tablespoon dry
Butter Buds

1. Steam Brussels sprouts until crisp tender. (3 to 5 minutes)

2. In a nonstick skillet reduce ¼ cup chicken broth down to 1 tablespoon.

3. Mix dry Butter Buds with remaining ¼ cup chicken broth add to the pan and reduce by ½ .

4. Cut Brussels sprouts in half, add to pan and saute until all are well coated and hot.

Makes 4 servings.

Each serving contains:

49 calories
4 grams protein
10 grams carbohy-
drate
.5 grams fat
0 mgs.. cholesterol

122 mgs.. sodium
3 grams dietary
fiber
ADA Exchange Value
2 Vegetables

Cauliflower Au Gratin

1 large head fresh cauliflower (or 2 packages frozen, thawed)
1 cup nonfat milk
1 tablespoon corn starch or arrow-root
½ teaspoon freshly ground black pepper
¼ teaspoon cayenne pepper
2 ounces lowfat cheese, grated
2 tablespoons dry bread crumbs
2 tablespoons freshly grated parmesan cheese

1. Preheat oven to 350 degrees.

2. Cut cauliflower into small flowerettes, wash then steam until crisp tender (3 to 5 minutes).

3. In a medium sauce pan, mix milk, cornstarch, black and cayenne pepper until cornstarch has dissolved.

4. Heat over medium heat until mixture comes to a boil and thickens.

5. Remove from heat and stir in cheese until melted and well mixed. Add cauliflower and gently toss to coat all the pieces.

6. Place cauliflower in a baking or souffle dish that has been sprayed with a nonstick spray. Pour cheese sauce over cauliflower.

7. Sprinkle bread crumbs and parmesan cheese over top and bake 15 to 20 minutes, or until mixture is hot and bubbly.

Makes 4 servings.

Each serving contains:

110 calories
9 grams protein
11 grams carbohydrate
4 grams fat
12 mgs.. cholesterol
191 mgs.. sodium

2 grams dietary fiber
ADA Exchange Value
½ Starch/Bread
1 Lean Meat
1 Vegetable

Cabbage Confetti

3 cups fresh red cabbage, coarsely chopped

2 cups fresh green beans, cut in thin slices

1 large carrot, coarsely grated

1 tablespoon fresh onion, chopped

½ cup Vinaigrette Dressing (page 61)

1. Steam cabbage and green beans until crisp tender. (2 to 3 minutes)

2. Saute onion lightly in a nonstick skillet sprayed with a nonstick spray, add cabbage, green beans, carrot, and Vinaigrette Dressing.

3. Cook over low heat 3 to 5 minutes, or until heated through.

Makes 4 servings.

Each serving contains:

81 calories
2 grams protein
12 grams carbohy-
drate
4 grams fat
0 mgs.. cholesterol

27 mgs.. sodium
3 grams dietary
fiber
ADA Exchange Value
2 Vegetables
1 Fat

Glazed Carrots

½ pound carrots,
peeled and sliced
diagonally
1 tablespoon apple
juice concentrate

1 teaspoon corn
starch
1 teaspoon dry
mustard
¼ cup water

1. Steam carrots until crisp tender (3 to 5 minutes)

2. In a nonstick skillet combine apple juice concentrate, corn starch, mustard and water, heat and stir continuously until thickened and smooth.

3. Add carrots, toss until well coated and heated.

Makes 4 servings.

Each serving contains:

34 calories
0 grams protein
8 grams carbohy-
drate
0 grams fat
0 mgs.. cholesterol
20 mgs.. sodium

2 grams dietary
fiber
ADA Exchange Value
1½ Vegetables

Artichokes

4 medium artichokes
1 clove garlic

1 lemon
1 teaspoon dill

1. Cut the tops and stems off artichokes, trim off the thorns with kitchen shears. (this gives them a much prettier appearance)

2. Fill a large pot ¼ full with water, bring to a boil.

3. Peel the garlic clove, add to the water.

4. Cut the lemon in half squeeze the juice into the water then drop the lemon in the water.

5. Add dill.

6. Put the artichokes into the boiling water, reduce heat, cover, simmer for 45 minutes or until you can insert a fork easily in the heart.

Makes 4 servings

Each Artichoke Contains:

61 calories	4 grams dietary fiber
3 grams protein	
15 grams carbohy-drate	**ADA Exchange Value**
0 grams fat	3 Vegetables
0 mgs.. cholesterol	
80 mgs.. sodium	

Julienne Carrots and Zucchini

2 **medium carrots**	½ **teaspoon dill weed**
2 **medium zucchini**	
2 **teaspoons corn oil**	
margarine	

1. Steam carrots until crisp tender. This makes them easier to cut. Cut carrots and zucchini into Julienne pieces (⅛ by 2 inches).

2. Melt margarine in medium size skillet, add dill, carrots, zucchini, and gently toss.

3. Turn off heat, cover and let stand 2 to 3 minutes, serve.

Makes 4 servings.

Each serving contains:

45 calories	14 mgs.. sodium
1 gram protein	2 grams dietary
6 grams carbohy-	fiber
drate	**ADA Exchange Value**
2 grams fat	1 Vegetable
0 mgs.. cholesterol	½ Fat

Mushrooms and Chinese Peas

4 cups sliced
mushrooms
2 cups Chinese pea
pods

¼ cup chicken broth

1. Reduce chicken broth to 2 tablespoons in a medium nonstick skillet.

2. Add mushrooms and saute until tender.

3. Add Chinese pea pods and stir 30 seconds.

4. Turn off heat cover and let stand 3 minutes before serving.

Makes 4 servings.

Each serving contains:

51 calories
4 grams protein
9 grams carbohy-
drate
0 grams fat
0 mgs.. cholesterol

53 mgs.. sodium
6 grams dietary
fiber
ADA Exchange Value
2 Vegetable

Panned Green Beans

2 cups fresh green beans with stems removed (frozen, thawed may be used)

¼ cup liquid Butter Buds
½ teaspoon minced garlic

1. Steam green beans until tender (5 minutes)
2. Heat the liquid Butter Buds in a medium nonstick skillet.
3. Add garlic and cook lightly.
4. Add green beans and toss until well coated and hot.

Makes 4 servings.

Each serving contains:

23 calories
1 gram protein
5 grams carbohy-drate
0 gram fat

0 mgs.. cholesterol
2 mgs.. sodium
1 gram dietary fiber
ADA Exchange Value
1 Vegetable

Ratatouille

Servings are large, and chock-full of low calorie vegetables.

1 large onion, sliced	1/4 cup tomato paste
4 medium zucchini, sliced	1/2 teaspoon minced garlic
1 green or red sweet pepper, seeded and sliced	1/4 cup fresh parsley, chopped
1 eggplant, peeled and cubed	2 teaspoons sweet basil
4 tomatoes, chopped in large pieces	1 teaspoon oregano
	1/4 teaspoon black pepper

1. Combine all ingredients in a large saucepan.

2. Cook over medium heat until all vegetables are tender, stirring frequently.

3. Reduce heat, cover and simmer 10 to 15 minutes.

4. Remove cover and continue cooking until liquid has evaporated and mixture has thickened.

5. May be served hot or cold.

Makes 6 servings.

Each serving contains:

65 calories	19 mgs.. sodium
3 grams protein	4 grams dietary fiber
14 grams carbohydrate	**ADA Exchange Value**
0 grams fat	3 Vegetables
0 mgs.. cholesterol	

Savory Celery

This would be good added to a salad or a crudities tray.

I bunch fresh celery, separated
I cup chicken broth

¼ cup Sherry Dressing (page 59)

1. Wash celery and cut in even pieces (about 1").

2. Place celery and chicken broth in a large saucepan, bring to boil.

3. Reduce heat, cover and simmer for 5 minutes.

4. Drain celery and toss with Sherry dressing.

5. Serve warm or well chilled.

Makes 4 servings.

Each Serving Contains:

30 calories
2 grams protein
4 grams carbohydrate
I gram fat
0 mgs.. cholesterol
273 mgs.. sodium

I grams dietary fiber
ADA Exchange Value
I Vegetable

Stuffed Tomatoes

**4 medium tomatoes
1 cup frozen petite
 peas
½ cup nonfat milk
2 teaspoons
 cornstarch**

**1 teaspoon liquid
 Butter Buds
dash of cayenne
 pepper**

1. Cut off top of each tomato. Carefully cut around the inside of each tomato, about ½ inch from the outside bottom make a small slit and cut the bottom part of the core. Spoon out pulp and seeds. (Reserve for use in tomato sauces.)

2. Steam peas until crisp tender.

3. Mix milk, cornstarch, Butter Buds, and pepper in a small saucepan, heat stirring constantly until thickened.

4. Combine peas in the sauce and spoon into the tomatoes.

5. Warm in oven for 5 minutes at 350 degrees just before serving.

Makes 4 servings.

Each serving contains:

**74 calories
4 grams protein
14 grams carbohy-
 drate
0 grams fat
.5 mgs.. cholesterol**

**61 mgs.. sodium
4 grams dietary
 fiber
ADA Exchange Value
½ Starch/Bread
1 Vegetable**

Variations: add a dash of nutmeg or curry powder to the milk mixture and serve cold.

Sweet and Sour
Red Cabbage

This is better made a day ahead and heated or served cold.

4 cups fresh red cabbage, coarsely grated

1 small onion, chopped

¼ cup lemon juice

½ cup fresh orange juice

2 tablespoons apple juice concentrate

½ cup chicken broth

1 tablespoon cornstarch or arrowroot

1. Steam cabbage until tender (3 to 5 minutes).

2. In a nonstick skillet reduce ¼ cup chicken broth to 1 tablespoon.

3. Add onion and saute until tender.

4. Mix lemon juice, orange juice, apple juice, remaining broth, and cornstarch until cornstarch is dissolved.

5. Pour mixture into skillet and stir until it comes to a boil and thickens.

6. Add cabbage and toss until well coated.

7. Put in covered container and refrigerate several hours or overnight if possible.

Makes 4 servings.

Each serving contains:

77 calories

2 grams protein

17 grams carbohydrate

0 grams fat

0 mgs.. cholesterol

106 mgs.. sodium

3 grams dietary fiber

ADA Exchange Value

2 Vegetable

½ Fruit

Zucchini Boats

4 medium zucchini
2 tablespoons to-
   mato paste
½ teaspoon Italian
   Blend (page 22)
1 clove fresh garlic,
   minced

¼ cup dry bread
   crumbs
2 tablespoons par-
   mesan cheese,
   freshly grated

1. Wash zucchini and cut in half lengthwise.

2. Steam until tender (3 minutes)

3. With a spoon scoop out zucchini pulp, leaving "shell" intact.

4. Place the pulp of the zucchini in a bowl and mash with a fork.

5. Mix in tomato paste, Italian Seasonings blend, and garlic.

6. Stuff mixture into "shells" and sprinkle each with bread crumbs and parmesan cheese.

7. Place under broiler until cheese and bread crumbs are brown.

Makes 4 servings.

Each serving contains.

56 calories
 3 grams protein
 8 grams carbohy-
    drate
 1 gram fat
 2 mgs. cholesterol
111 mgs. sodium

1 gram dietary fiber
ADA Exchange Value
 2 vegetables

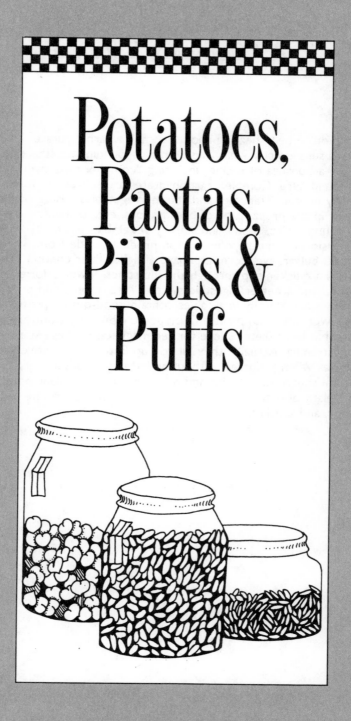

Potatoes, Pastas, Pilafs & Puffs

A "Complex Bonanza"

If you've been hearing about "complex carbohydrates" and aren't sure exactly what these strange-sounding substances are, well—a bonanza of recipes including "complex carbohydrates" can be found here. Complex carbohydrates are substances found chiefly in grains, legumes and starchy vegetables. Using whole grains in the preparation of breads, rolls, etc., and eating a variety of legumes, rice, pastas and starchy vegetables has multi-dimensional bonuses. Whole grain products made from whole wheat, bulgar, rye, corn, etc. have a higher fiber content. This means a quicker trip through the intestines, fewer calories absorbed and a better digestive system. Also, most grain products, legumes and starchy vegetables contain good-quality protein at a far lower cost than meat, fish or poultry protein. Contrary to what has been dieter's lore for seemingly eons, these starches are not fattening. Actually, they fill you up faster, are relatively low in calories when prepared without added fats or oils and are a good natural source of vitamins and minerals. So, enjoy your potato, eat that plate of pasta, spoon the rice onto your dish can be healthy happy, and satisfied.

PROPORTIONS AND COOKING TIMES FOR GRAINS

Grain (1 cup)	Water or Stock	Cooking Time	Cooked Amount
Barley	3 cups	1 hour 15 mins.	3½ cups
Brown rice	2 cups	1 hour	3 cups
Wild rice	3 cups	1 hour +	4 cups
Black beans	4 cups	1½ hours	2 cups
Garbanzos	4 cups	3 hours	2 cups
Kidney beans	3 cups	1½ hours	2 cups
Lentils & split peas	3 cups	1 hour	2¼ cups
Limas	2 cups	1½ hours	1¼ cups
Baby Limas	2 cups	1½ hours	1¾ cups
Pinto Beans	3 cups	2½ hours	2 cups
Red Beans	3 cups	3 hours	2 cups
Small White Beans	3 cups	1½ hours	2 cups

Oven Roasted Potatoes

4 small potatos, unpeeled, cut into   **quarters the long way**

1. Preheat oven to 450 degrees.

2. Place potato pieces on a nonstick baking sheet.

3. Bake for 20 minutes or until tender when pricked with a fork, and browned.

Makes 4 servings.

Each serving contains:

76 calories
2 grams protein
17 grams carbohy-
   drate
0 grams fat
0 mgs. cholesterol

3 mgs. sodium
2 grams dietary
   fiber
ADA Exchange Value
1 Starch/Bread

Oven Potato Chips

Bet you can't eat just one! For extra flavor try sprinkling them with garlic powder or herbs before baking.

**4 small potatos,
unpeeled, sliced
very thin**

1. Preheat oven to 450 degrees.
2. Spread potatos on a nonstick cookie sheet.
3. Bake until lightly browned 10 to 12 minutes.

Makes 4 servings.

Each Serving Contains:

76 calories	**0** mgs. cholesterol
2 grams protein	**3** mgs. sodium
17 grams carbohy-drate	**2** grams dietary fiber
0 grams fat	**ADA Exchange Value**
	1 Starch/Bread

Herbed Stuffed Potatos

4 small potatos, unpeeled
¼ cup nonfat milk
1 tablespoon parmesan cheese
2 tablespoons sour cream

1 green onion, chopped
¼ teaspoon Italian Blend (page 22)

1. Preheat oven to 350 degrees.

2. Bake potatos 45 minutes or until soft.

3. Make a slit in the potato, press open carefully and scoop out potato.

4. Mix potato with all other ingredients.

5. Put the filling into the 4 shells.

6. Bake at 350 for 10 minutes or until hot.

Makes 4 servings.

Each serving contains:

104 calories
4 grams protein
18 grams carbohydrate
2 grams fat
5 mgs. cholesterol

44 mgs. sodium
2 grams dietary fiber
ADA Exchange Value
1 Starch/Bread
½ Fat

Parslied Potatos

4 small red potatos,
unpeeled, sliced

fresh parsley,
minced

1. Steam potatos 10 minutes.
2. Arrange slices on serving plate.
3. Sprinkle with fresh parsley.

Makes 4 servings.

Each serving contains:

78 calories
2 grams protein
18 grams carbohy-
drate
0 grams fat

0 mgs. cholesterol
6 mgs. sodium
2 grams dietary
fiber
ADA Exchange Value
1 Starch/Bread

Potato Pie

This is a fun one to play with as you can use several different vegetables in the layering; i.e. shredded zucchini, red onions, green beans, broccoli, mushrooms, etc.

3 medium potatos, thinly sliced

2 medium carrots, grated

3 green onions, chopped including green tops

I can chicken broth reduced to I cup

I tablespoon chopped parsley

1. Preheat oven to 350 degrees.

2. Arrange 2 layers of potatos around a 9 inch pie or quiche pan that has been sprayed with a nonsitck coating.

3. Spread the carrots and onions over potatos.

4. Layer the remaining potatos on top.

5. Pour broth over top.

6. Cover and bake 40 minutes.

7. Uncover sprinkle parsley over top.

8. Bake uncovered 10 to 15 minutes.

9. Let stand 10 minutes, cut into pie shaped wedges.

Makes 4 servings.

Each serving contains:

145 calories
5 grams protein
30 grams carbohydrate
I gram fat
0 mgs. cholesterol

407 mgs. sodium
4 grams dietary fiber
ADA Exchange Value
2 Starch/Bread

Bulgar Pilaf

Bulgar is cracked wheat which, when cooked, is similar in appearance and texture to brown rice. It has its own unique flavor and aroma with the nutritional bonus of whole grain wheat.

1¾ cup chicken broth
½ onion, chopped
1 tablespoon parsley, minced
¼ cup carrot, shredded or chopped

¼ cup zucchini, shredded or chopped
1 cup bulgar wheat
¼ teaspoon cumin
dash of red chili pepper or cayenne

1. In a quart sauce pan reduce ¼ cup chicken broth to 1 tablespoon.

2. Add onion and brown.

3. Add parsley, carrot, zucchini, and the remaining chicken broth and bring to boil.

4. Add bulgar, cumin and red pepper.

5. Cover, reduce heat and simmer for 15 minutes or until all liquid is absorbed.

6. Fluff with a fork.

Makes 4 servings.

Each serving contains:

120 calories
5 grams protein
24 grams carbohydrate
1 gram fat

0 mgs. cholesterol
229 mgs. sodium
1 gram dietary fiber
ADA Exchange Value
1½ Starch/Bread

Brown Rice Pilaf

2 1/4 cups vegetable broth or water
1 onion, sliced
1/4 pound fresh mushrooms, sliced
1 cup brown rice
1 teaspoon oregano
1 tablespoon soy sauce
1/4 cup sliced almonds, toasted

1. In a large nonstick skillet cook onion and mushrooms in 1/4 cup broth until all liquid is gone.

2. Add rice, soy sauce, oregano and rest of broth and bring to boil.

3. Turn down heat, cover and simmer 45 minutes or until all liquid is absorbed.

4. Stir toasted almonds into rice when ready to serve.

Makes 6 servings.

Each serving contains:

156 calories
4 grams protein
28 grams carbohydrate
3 grams fat
0 mgs. cholesterol

176 mgs. sodium
2 grams dietary fiber
ADA Exchange Value
2 Starch/Bread

Pita Bread

2 cups warm water (105 to 115 degrees)

2 tablespoons fructose

2 tablespoons olive oil

1 tablespoon or 1 package dry yeast

4½ cups whole wheat flour

1. Preheat oven to 500 degrees. (read #17 before preheating)

2. Dissolve fructose in 2 cups warm water.

3. Beat in oil.

4. Sprinkle yeast on top of water mixture, stir to mix.

5. Let rest 10 minutes until frothy.

6. Put 1 cup flour in a mixing bowl.

7. Pour yeast mixture into flour and beat with a mixer 5 minutes.

8. Gradually add enough flour to form a stiff dough.

9. Turn out onto a lightly floured board and knead until smooth and no longer sticky (5 or 10 minutes)

10. Turn into lightly oiled bowl, rub the top with olive oil so it doesn't dry out.

11. Cover with a kitchen towel or plastic wrap and let rise in a warm spot for about 1½ hours or until double in bulk.

12. Punch down and knead until air bubbles are gone.

13. Roll into a long thin log and cut into 18 sections.

14. Roll each section into approximately 6 inch circle on a floured board.

15. Place rounds on cookie sheets, 2 inches apart.

16. Cover with a towel or plastic wrap and let rise until double in bulk. (30 to 40 minutes)

17. Bake 4 to 5 minutes.

a. Gas ovens place cookie sheet on the oven floor.

b. Electric ovens, remove the upper heating element (most snap out for easy cleaning) place cookie sheet on the lowest rack.

Makes 18 servings.

Each Serving Contains:

120 calories
4 grams protein
23 grams carbohy-
drate
2 grams fat
0 mgs. cholesterol

1 mg. sodium
4 grams dietary
fiber
ADA Exchange Value
1½ **Starch/Bread**

Whole Wheat Yeast Rolls

These rolls freeze well, and if dry, reheat in a steamer about 30 seconds.

½ cup nonfat milk, scalded (cool to 105 to 115 degrees)

¾ cup warm water (105 to 115 degrees)

2 tablespoons fructose

1 tablespoon or 1 package active dry yeast

2 tablespoons corn oil margarine

1 whole egg

1 cup unbleached flour

2½ cups whole wheat flour

1 egg white mixed with 2 tablespoons water

1. Melt margarine in scalded milk, add water making sure temperature stays between 105 to 115 degrees.

2. Stir in fructose until dissolved.

3. Sprinkle yeast on top, whisk until well blended and allow to set for 10 minutes.

4. Beat egg and whisk into mixture.

5. Add 1 cup unbleached flour and beat for 5 minutes with mixer at high speed.

6. Gradually add remaining flour, turn out onto floured board and knead 5 to 10 minutes until smooth, elastic and no longer sticky.

7. Allow to rise 1½ hours in a greased bowl covered with tea towel or plastic wrap, in a warm spot in the kitchen.

8. Punch down and roll into 2 dozen balls, (about the size of golf balls)

9. Place on cookie sheet lined with waxed paper, brush with egg white mixture, and allow to rise 1 hour.

10. Preheat oven to 450 degrees.

11. Bake 12 to 15 minutes.

Makes 24 rolls.

Each Roll Contains:

78 calories
3 grams protein
14 grams carbohy-
   drate
1 gram fat
12 mgs. cholesterol

19 mgs. sodium
2 grams dietary
   fiber
ADA Exchange Value
1 Starch/Bread

Main Dishes

THE MAIN EVENT

*D*inner is served! The entrees presented here are quick, nutritious and eye-appealing. Yet, each is suitable for a formal gathering, romantic candlelight supper or crowd-sized gathering. Many can be made ahead and refrigerated or frozen for a fast trip from oven to table, next week or next month. You'll find adaptations of family favorites which, for the most part, are lower in calories, cholesterol and salt than their traditional counterparts, without sacrificing flavor or appetite-appeal.

Barbecued Chicken

2 large whole chicken breasts, boned, split and skinned (1 pound) Chicken or beef marinade (page 129)

1. Marinate chicken breast in the marinade overnight or at least 4 to 6 hours.

2. Barbecue or broil the breast until done, they cook quickly about 20 minutes so be careful not to over cook.

Makes 4 servings.

Each Serving Contains:

154 calories	324 mgs. sodium
27 grams protein	0 grams dietary fiber
1 grams carbohydrate	**ADA Exchange Value**
4 grams fat	4 Lean Meat
73 mgs. cholesterol	

Chicken Breast Supreme

- 2 whole chicken breasts, boned, skinned and split (1 pound raw)
- 1/4 cup whole wheat pastry flour
- 2 cups chicken broth
- 2 teaspoons cornstarch
- 1/2 cup dry white wine or dry vermouth
- 8 mushrooms, sliced
- 1/4 cup sour cream
- 1/4 cup cold water
- 1/4 cup chopped parsley

1. Reduce 1/4 cup chicken broth to 1 tablespoon in a large non-stick skillet.

2. Saute mushrooms until tender, remove from skillet and set aside.

3. Add 1/4 cup chicken broth to skillet and reduce to 2 tablespoons.

4. Coat each 1/2 chicken breast in flour.

5. Brown each breast well on both sides, (you may need to add more chicken broth as you go).

6. Add the wine and remaining broth, cover and simmer until chicken is done (about 20 minutes).

7. Remove chicken breast and keep warm.

8. Dissolve cornstarch in 1/4 cup cold water.

9. Add to the skillet and cook to thicken.

10. Stir in sour cream and cook just enough to heat through.

11. To serve spoon sauce over chicken, top with mushrooms and parsley.

Makes 4 servings.

Each serving contains:

235 calories	7 grams fat
32 grams protein	85 mgs. cholesterol
8 grams carbohydrate	272 mgs. sodium
	1 gram dietary fiber

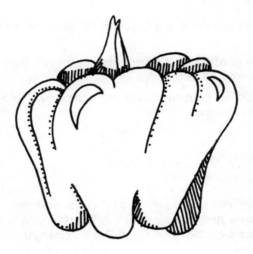

Chicken Cacciatore

2 whole large chicken breasts, boned, split and skinned

⅓ cup Crunchy Croutons, crushed (page 137)

¼ cup chicken broth

2 cups Marinara Sauce (page) 131

1. Place crushed croutons in a bag, add chicken and shake to cover.

2. In a medium nonstick skillet heat chicken broth. Reduce heat, and brown chicken on both sides.

3. Pour Marinara Sauce over, cover and simmer 20 to 30 minutes or until chicken is done.

Makes 4 servings.

Each Serving Contains:

211 calories
27 grams protein
15 grams carbohydrate
5 grams fat
64 mgs. cholesterol

619 mgs. sodium
1 gram dietary fiber
ADA Exchange Value
3 Lean Meat
2 Vegetable

Cornish Game Hens

2 Cornish game hens
1 orange

1¼ cup Orange Sauce (page 133)
4 slices of orange

1. Preheat oven to 350 degrees.

2. Cut each hen in half, wash and pat dry.

3. Cut orange in quarters and squeeze juice of ¼ orange on each half hen.

4. Place the ¼ orange under the halved hen. Place each on a roasting pan and bake for 1 hour.

5. After ½ hour baste with ¼ cup of the Orange Sauce.

6. To serve, pour ¼ cup orange sauce over each hen and garnish with twisted orange slices.

Makes 4 servings.

Each Serving Contains:

203 calories
26 grams protein
12 grams carbohydrate
4 grams fat
64 mgs. cholesterol

446 mgs. sodium
1 gram dietary fiber
ADA Exchange Value
3 Lean Meat
1 Fruit

Pepper Pots

4 large green pep-
pers
½ pound ground tur-
key, raw
1 cup brown rice,
cooked
½ cup onion,
chopped

½ teaspoon freshly
ground black pep-
per
1 teaspoon Italian
Blend (page 22)
2 cups Marinara
Sauce (page 131)

1. Preheat oven to 350 degrees.

2. Cut circular opening in top of peppers, wash and remove seeds.

3. Poach peppers in boiling water or steam for 5 minutes.

4. Mix together turkey, onions, rice, seasonings and 1 cup of Marinara Sauce.

5. Stuff each pepper with ¼ of the mixture.

6. Place in covered baking dish and bake 50 to 60 minutes.

7. Put ¼ cup hot Marinara Sauce on each before serving.

Makes 4 servings.

Each Serving Contains:

270 calories
18 grams protein
29 grams carbohy-
drate
10 grams fat
49 mgs. cholesterol

499 mgs. sodium
3 grams dietary
fiber
ADA Exchange Value
1 Starch/Bread
2 Lean Meat
2 Vegetable
1 Fat

Turkey Chili

1 pound bag of dried beans: black, pinto, navy, or mixed. (soak beans overnight, rinse, then cook in chicken, beef or vegetable broth until barely tender.)

1 tablespoon olive oil

2 medium onions chopped

1 clove garlic minced

2 bell peppers chopped

½ teaspoon oregano

¼ teaspoon cumin

3 teaspoons chili powder

1 teaspoon ground red pepper (or to taste)

1 pound ground turkey, raw

1-28 oz. can diced tomatoes

1-15 oz. can tomato sauce

1. Heat a large dutch oven, add olive oil.

2. Saute onion, garlic until yellow.

3. Add bell peppers and seasonings.

4. Add ground turkey and cook constantly stirring until done.

5. Add tomatoes, tomato sauce, and drained beans.

6. Simmer 1 hour.

Makes 6 - 7 servings.

Each Serving Contains:

327 calories
26 grams protein
30 grams carbohydrate
13 grams fat
63 mgs. cholesterol
281 mgs. sodium

6 grams dietary fiber

ADA Exchange Value
2 Starch/Bread
2 Lean Meat
2 Fat

Baked Sole With Shrimp and Asparagus

4 sole filets
(3 ounces each)
4 large uncooked
shrimp
4 asparagus tips,
steamed to crisp
tender

fresh dill sprigs
(dried dill weed
may be used)
1 lemon paprika

1. Preheat oven to 350 degrees.

2. Shell, clean, devein and butterfly shrimp.

3. Place a shrimp in the center of each sole filet.

4. Put an asparagus tip on top of the shrimp and roll jelly roll-style, secure with a toothpick.

5. Place fish rolls in a baking dish, squeeze lemon juice over, sprinkle with fresh dill and paprika.

6. Bake for 20 minutes or until fish flakes.

Makes 4 servings.

Each serving contains:

204 calories
31 grams protein
4 grams carbohy-
drate
7 grams fat
37 mgs. cholesterol

237 mgs. sodium
0 grams dietary
fiber
ADA Exchange Value
4 Lean Meat

Fiesta Fish

2 pounds fresh white fish

1 cup chopped tomatoes

1 whole green pepper, chopped

2 tablespoons red onion, chopped

3 tablespoons lemon juice

1 tablespoon olive oil

1 teaspoon basil

½ teaspoon freshly ground black pepper

¼ teaspoon chili powder

1. Preheat oven to 350 degrees.

2. Heat olive oil in a nonstick skillet and saute green pepper, onion, and tomatoes 1 to 2 minutes to soften.

3. Remove from heat add lemon juice, basil, pepper, and chili powder.

4. Place fish in a baking dish that has been sprayed with a nonstick spray.

5. Spoon vegetable mixture over fish, cover and bake 25 to 30 minutes, or until fish flakes with a fork.

Makes 6 servings.

Each Serving Contains:

321 calories

33 grams protein

5 grams carbohydrate

11 grams fat

37 mgs. cholesterol

97 mgs. sodium

1 gram dietary fiber

ADA Exchange Value

4 Lean Meat

1 Vegetable

Linguini With Clam Sauce

15 ounce diced toma-
toes in juice
1 6½ ounce can
chopped clams
1 clove garlic
minced
2 tablespoons
capers

3 tablespoons fresh
parsley chopped
1 teaspoon olive oil
½ teaspoon freshly
ground black
pepper
½ pound cooked and
drained pasta

1. Heat olive oil in a large nonstick skillet.

2. Saute garlic and capers for 1 minute.

3. Add tomatoes, parsley, pepper, and clams, simmer for 5 minutes uncovered.

4. Toss with pasta and serve.

Makes 4 servings.

Each Serving Contains:

141 calories
8 grams protein
23 grams carbohy-
drate
2 grams fat
29 mgs. cholesterol

35 mgs. sodium
1 gram dietary fiber
ADA Exchange Value
1 Starch/Bread
1 Lean Meat
1 Vegetable

Lamb Kebobs

1 pound very lean
 lamb, cubed
 Marinade for lamb
 (page 130)
12 mushrooms

1½ bell peppers, cut
 into 12 cubes
12 pearl onions or 12
 slices of onion
4 skewers

1. Marinate the lamb cubes in the Marinade for at least 4 hours, it's best when marinated overnight.

2. Alternate the ingredients on the skewer, starting and finishing with mushrooms.

3. Barbecue or broil, using Marinade to baste when the kebobs are cooking.

Makes 4 servings.

Each serving contains:

188 calories
 16 grams protein
 6 grams carbohy-
 drate
 11 grams fat
 53 mgs. cholesterol

55 mgs. sodium
 1 gram dietary fiber
ADA Exchange Value
 2 Lean Meat
 1 Vegetable
 1 Fat

Meatballs Marinara

½ pound very lean ground beef
1 whole egg
½ teaspoon garlic powder
¼ teaspoon black pepper
2 teaspoons parsley, freshly chopped
1 tablespoon parmesan cheese
¼ cup Crunchy Croutons (page 137)
2 cups Marinara Sauce (page 131)

1. Mix all ingredients except Marinara Sauce in a bowl.

2. Form into 16 walnut-sized meatballs.

3. Brown meatballs on all sides in a nonstick pan sprayed with a nonstick spray.

4. Add Marinara Sauce, cover and simmer for 30 minutes.

Makes 4 servings.

Each Serving Contains:

250 calories
20 grams protein
15 grams carbohydrate
13 grams fat
118 mgs. cholesterol

585 mgs. sodium
1 gram dietary fiber
ADA Exchange Value
2 Lean Meat
3 Vegetable
1 Fat

Flank Steak Roulade

1 pound flank steak	½ can water chest-
1 box frozen spin-	nuts sliced
ach, thawed and	1 recipe Beef Mari-
steamed 1 minute	nade (page 129)

1. Trim any fat from flank steak and score on both sides (shallow diagonal slices).

2. Marinate in Beef Marinade several hours or overnight.

3. Drain spinach thoroughly and squeeze to eliminate as much moisture as possible.

4. Spread spinach evenly over steak.

5. Arrange water chestnuts on top of spinach and carefully roll up, jelly roll-style. Secure with toothpicks.

6. Slice into 8 even pieces.

7. Brush with marinade and broil or barbecue 5 to 7 minutes on each side or until cooked to desired "doneness."

Makes 4 servings.

Each serving contains:

190 calories	347 mgs. sodium
28 grams protein	1 gram dietary fiber
5 grams carbohy-drate	ADA Exchange Value
6 grams fat	3 Lean Meat
20 mgs. cholesterol	1 Vegetable

Pasta Primavera

½ cup carrots, grated

1 cup zucchini, grated or diced

3 large green onions, diced, green part only

½ teaspoon minced garlic

1 cut broccoli flowerettes (steam 3 to 5 minutes)

½ cup small peas (steam 3 to 5 minutes)

1 tablespoon chopped parsley

½ teaspoon Italian Blend (page 22)

1 cup nonfat milk

2 teaspoons cornstarch

1 tablespoons liquid Butter Buds

¼ cup sour cream

½ cup grated parmesan cheese pepper to taste

4 cups cooked pasta

1. Spray a large nonstick skillet with a nonstick coating. Saute carrots, zucchini, onions and garlic until tender.

2. Add cornstarch to milk and mix until dissolved.

3. Add liquid Butter Buds to milk.

4. Stir milk mixture into sauteed vegetables, stir over medium heat until sauce thickens.

5. Stir in sour cream, parsley and Italian Blend.

6. Add broccoli and peas, stir in gently.

7. Place pasta that has been well drained in a bowl.

8. Pour sauce over pasta, add parmesan cheese and toss thoroughly.

9. Serve immediately.

Makes 4 servings.

Each serving contains:

313 calories
15 grams protein

59 grams carbohydrate
4 grams fat

181 mgs. cholesterol
185 mgs. sodium
3 grams dietary
   fiber

ADA Exchange Value
2½ Starch/Bread
3 Vegetable
1 Fat

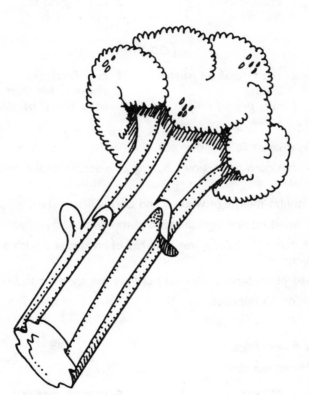

Tamale Pie

Cornbread:

1 cup corn meal
1 cup whole wheat flour
1 tablespoon baking powder
1 tablespoon fructose

1 cup cooked and drained corn kernels
1 cup nonfat milk
2 egg whites
2 tablespoons corn oil

Topping:

2 cups cooked pinto beans
1 cup green chile salsa

1 cup farmers cheese, broken into small pieces

1. Preheat oven to 350 degrees.

2. Combine corn meal, flour, baking powder, fructose, and corn in a large bowl.

3. Mix nonfat milk, egg whites, and corn oil together.

4. Add liquid to dry ingredients and mix well.

5. Pour into a 9" baking pan that has been sprayed with a non-stick spray.

6. Spread pinto beans, salsa, and cheese evenly over the top.

7. Bake for 35 minutes.

Makes 6 servings.

Each serving contains:

355 calories
18 grams protein
51 grams carbohydrate
17 grams fat
10 mgs. cholesterol
401 mgs. sodium

4 grams dietary fiber

ADA Exchange Value
3 Starch/Bread
1 Lean Meat
1 Vegetable
1 Fat

Moussaka

Makes large servings, lots of vegetables and very low in calories.

1 medium eggplant, peeled and sliced in 1/4 inch rounds	1 tablespoon tomato paste
1/4 cup chicken broth	1/8 teaspoon allspice
1 clove garlic minced	1/8 teaspoon nutmeg
1/2 medium onion, chopped	1 cup lowfat ricotta cheese
1 cup zucchini, grated	1/4 cup parmesan cheese
1 14 1/2 ounce can diced tomatoes in juice	Fat Free White Sauce*

1. Preheat oven to 350 degrees.

2. Steam eggplant 3 to 5 minutes and set aside on paper towels.

3. Reduce broth to 1 tablespoon in a large nonstick skillet.

4. Saute garlic, onion, and zucchini until tender.

5. Add tomatoes, tomato paste, allspice, and nutmeg, simmer for 15 minutes.

6. Spray a 9 inch baking pan with a nonstick coating. Layer half of the eggplant.

7. Spread the vegetable sauce over eggplant, then layer remaining eggplant.

8. Top with ricotta cheese.

9. Spread the Fat Free White sauce* over the ricotta cheese and sprinkle with the parmesan cheese.

10. Bake for 45 minutes, let stand for 10 minutes before serving.

Makes 4 servings.

* See Fat Free White sauce recipe on the following page.

Fat Free White Sauce

1 teaspoon dry
Butter Buds
1 ½ cups
nonfat milk
dash of white
pepper

3 tablespoons of
Cream of Rice
cereal

1. Combine milk, white pepper, and Butter Buds in a saucepan and bring to a boil.

2. Add cream of rice and stir for 30 sec.

3. Remove from heat, cover and let stand for 5 minutes.

4. Beat until smooth with a wire whisk.

Makes 4 servings.

Each serving contains:*

210 calories
16 grams protein
22 grams carbohy-
drate
8 grams fat
25 mgs. cholesterol
399 mgs. sodium

3 grams dietary
fiber
ADA Exchange Value
1 Lean Meat
3 Vegetable
½ Nonfat Milk
1 Fat*

* This nutritional breakdown represents 1 combined serving of Moussaka with the White sauce poured over it.

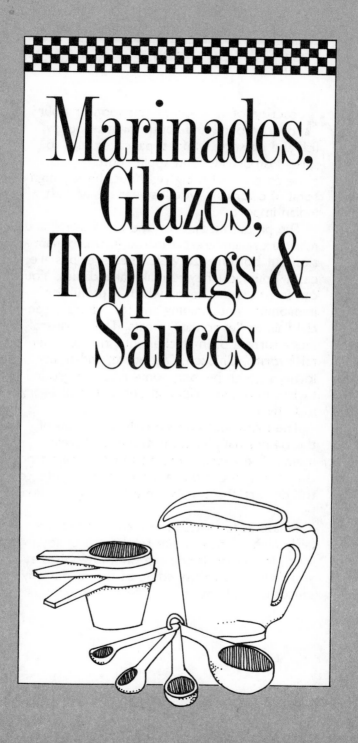

Marinades,
Glazes,
Toppings &
Sauces

IT'S IN THE SAUCE

A section of serendipity to spoon or pour over, around and about meats, poultry, fish and desserts, waffles, pancakes, and to spread on breads. The apple chutney—so close to the real thing (without the sky-high total of calories)—you'll swear it's an East Indian import.

The pasta sauces, both the quick sauce and marinara sauce, are calculated in small quantities, but both freeze well. These recipes are easily doubled (they're make-aheadable). You can freeze some items, which is useful for impromptu entertaining and for adding a special flair to "everyday" meats. The marinara sauce turns a plain chicken into the continental favorite, Chicken Cacciatore, and transforms a green pepper, some rice and ground turkey into a colorful and out-of-the-ordinary main dish.

The marinades contain only a fraction of the oil normally found in traditional treatments. The extra calories and fat missing from the marinade can mean, perhaps, a venture to the dessert chapter for an exciting grand finale.

Please note that some of the recipes are fairly high in sodium due to the use of soy sauce for flavor. If you are on a low salt diet you may want to use some of the milder soy sauces or none at all.

Marinade (Chicken or Beef)

Juice of 1 lemon
2 tablespoons soy sauce
2 tablespoons water
1/4 teaspoon garlic, minced

1/4 teaspoon ground ginger
1/2 teaspoon paprika

1. Combine all ingredients.

Enough to marinate 1 pound of chicken or beef.

One Recipe Contains:

42 calories
4 grams protein
9 grams carbohydrate
0 grams fat
0 mgs. cholesterol
2060 mgs. sodium
0 grams dietary fiber

ADA Exchange Value
negligible calories per serving

Marinade (Lamb)

Juice of ½ lemon
 ½ teaspoon garlic,
  minced
 1 teaspoon olive oil
 ⅛ teaspoon
  coriander

⅛ teaspoon cumin
⅛ teaspoon cayenne
  pepper

1. Combine all ingredients.

Enough to marinate 1 pound of lamb.

One Recipe Contains:

138 calories
  0 grams protein
  6 grams carbohy-
   drate
 14 grams fat
  0 mgs. cholesterol
  2 mgs. sodium

0 grams dietary
 fiber
ADA Exchange Value
 negligible calories
 per serving

Marinade Sauce

A good basic sauce, make ahead and freeze in 1 cup containers to have on hand when a recipe calls for Marinara Sauce.

1 medium onion, thinly sliced
1 teaspoon garlic, minced
1 teaspoon olive oil
1 -pound 12-ounce can tomato puree
1 -pound 12-ounce can peeled whole tomatoes
1 -pound 12-ounce can tomato sauce

2 ounces black olives, sliced (one small can)
2 tablespoons parmesan cheese
¼ teaspoon pepper
½ teaspoon Italian Blend (page 22)
1 tablespoon parsley, minced

1. Saute onion and garlic in olive oil in a large pan.

2. Add the rest of the ingredients, cover and simmer for 3 hours.

3. If sauce becomes too thick add water.

Makes 14 -½ cup servings.

Each serving contains:

70 calories
3 grams protein
13 grams carbohydrate
2 grams fat
0 mgs. cholesterol

488 mgs. sodium
1 gram dietary fiber
ADA Exchange Value
2½ Vegetable

Quick Tomato Sauce With Sweet Basil

(for pasta)

½ cup onion chopped
½ teaspoon garlic, minced
1 teaspoon olive oil
1 pound 12-ounce can peeled, crushed tomatoes

2 teaspoons dried sweet basil, crushed

1. Saute onion and garlic in olive oil in a large pan.
2. Add tomatoes and basil, simmer for 15 minutes.

Makes 4½ cup servings.

Each serving contains:

58 calories
2 grams protein
11 grams carbohydrate
1 gram fat
0 mgs. cholesterol

322 mgs. sodium
2 grams dietary fiber
ADA Exchange Value
2 Vegetable

Orange Sauce

1 **can chicken broth**
2 **oranges**
3 **teaspoons cornstarch**
1 **teaspoon freshly grated orange rind**

2 **tablespoons Contreau**

1. Reduce broth to 1 cup.

2. Juice the 2 oranges.

3. Add cornstarch to juice, stir until dissolved.

4. Stir into reduced broth, stir over medium heat until slightly thickened.

5. Add grated orange rind and Contreau and stir in.

Makes 4 servings.

One serving = 1/4 cup.

Each serving contains:

50 **calories**
3 **grams protein**
6 **grams carbohy-drate**
0 **grams fat**
0 **mgs. cholesterol**

388 **mgs. sodium**
0 **grams dietary fiber**
ADA Exchange Value
1/2 **Starch/Bread**

Raspberry Sauce

12 ounce bag of fro-
zen unsweetened
raspberries
¼ cup apple juice
concentrate

2 teaspoons
cornstarch
2 packets Equal
(or 1 tablespoon
fructose)

1. Combine all ingredients except Equal and cook over medium heat until sauce thickens (about 10 minutes).

2. Remove from heat, add Equal and stir.

3. Serve hot or cold.

Makes approximately 1 cup.

1 serving = 3 tablespoons.

Each serving contains:

60 calories
0 grams protein
15 grams carbohy-
drate
0 grams fat
0 mgs. cholesterol

1 mg. sodium
1 gram dietary fiber
ADA Exchange Value
1 Fruit

Strawberry Apple Butter

This is a good, basic sauce to keep on hand. It can be used to spruce up many different foods and makes a lovely gift. Inspired by our friend, Jeanne Jones.

- **6 medium apples, unpeeled, cored and thinly sliced**
- **1 cup apple juice concentrate**
- **1 ½ teaspoons cinnamon**
- **½ teaspoon allspice**
- **¼ teaspoon ground cloves**

- **1 pound bag frozen unsweetened strawberries, thawed**
- **1 to 2 packets of Equal (or 1 tablespoon fructose)**

1. Combine apples, apple juice and spices in a large saucepan.

2. Bring to boil then simmer 20 to 25 minutes until very soft.

3. Add strawberries and simmer 5 minutes.

4. Put in a food processor or blender, add Equal and blend until very smooth.

1 serving = 1½ tablespoons.

Each serving contains:

- **61 calories**
- **0 grams protein**
- **16 grams carbohydrate**
- **0 grams fat**

- **0 mgs. cholesterol**
- **1 mg. sodium**
- **1 gram dietary fiber**
- **ADA Exchange Value**
- **1 Fruit**

Judy's Chutney
This makes a great hostess gift.

5 cups green apples, cored and diced (medium apples)

½ cup onion, diced (1 medium onion)

½ cup dried figs, chopped

½ cup dried apricots, chopped

1 cup raisins

¾ cup fructose

1 cup malt vinegar (or cider vinegar)

¾ teaspoon ground nutmeg

¾ teaspoon allspice

¾ teaspoon ground cloves

¾ teaspoon ground ginger

¼ to ½ teaspoon crushed hot red pepper flakes

1. Put all ingredients in a large pot, bring to boil, simmer uncovered 1 hour, stirring occasionally.

2. Let cool and put in 5 air tight containers (1 cup each). Refrigerate or freeze.

You can keep them in the freezer and take them out as you need them, although it will keep for a month without freezing.

Makes 5 cups.

1 serving = 2 tablespoons.

Each serving contains:

23 calories

0 grams protein

6 grams carbohydrate

0 grams fat

0 mgs. cholesterol

1 mg. sodium

.5 grams dietary fiber

ADA Exchange Value

⅓ Fruit

Crunchy Croutons

Ever wonder what to do with those last few slices of bread in the loaf that somehow become wrinkled, stiff or dry? Well, as a great money saver and tasty topping maker, with a few extra minutes, these dry bread slices can be converted into Crunchy Croutons. Store them in your "pantry" in an airtight jar or plastic container with a tight fitting lid.

**2 slices dry whole
grain bread
garlic powder,
basil, oregano
to taste**

1. Preheat oven to 250 degrees.

2. Cut bread into small cubes and place on a nonstick cookie sheet.

3. Sprinkle lightly with garlic powder, basil and/or oregano to taste.

4. Bake until lightly browned and crunchy, about 10 to 15 minutes.

Makes 4 servings.

One serving = ¼ cup.

Each serving contains:

31 calories	0 mgs. cholesterol
1 gram protein	79 mgs. sodium
6 grams carbohydrate	1 gram dietary fiber
.5 gram fat	**ADA Exchange Value**
	½ Starch/Bread

Desserts

SUGAR IS SWEET

Sugar *is* sweet and has a taste that attracts most of us. White sugar as we know it has gained the reputation of being a "poison" of sorts. It is a commonly used additive or ingredient in a rainbow variety of foods we eat. The truth is—*sugar* is *sugar!* It is also true that refined white sugar or even crystalline fructose has no particular redeeming nutritional qualities—often referred to as "empty calories." But brown sugar, raw sugar, honey, syrups or molasses are still sugars, too. They are a *bit* more unrefined, but have an insignificant amount of vitamins and minerals. In fact, sugar isn't even very high in calories (about 16 calories per teaspoon of granulated sugar) compared to fats or oils (about 45 calories per teaspoon).

Sugars have different levels of sweetness. For example, lactose (a milk sugar) in its pure form doesn't taste very sweet, while fructose (fruit sugar) tastes sweeter than sucrose (ordinary table sugar). This means less can be used to obtain a desired sweetness.

In this book we have used fructose, honey, molasses, concentrated apple juice or orange juice, and a product called Equal. All are used in quite small quantities and are calculated into each recipe's nutritional analysis. We do not profess to say that carte blanche use of simple sugars is okay; rather, when used appropriately, sugar serves to enhance flavor, texture or overall palatability of the foods in which it is used. We do not feel that one sweetener is better than another. Each has

168 special properties which make it useful in certain recipes and not in others. (For example, the Gingerbread recipe would require much more sugar for flavor than molasses.) Equal is approximately 200 times sweeter than sugar and contains very few calories. But it does not retain its sweetness when heated. So we have not used it in baked goods for that reason.

We have avoided using saccharin because we feel people should generally cut down on it's use. It's a little tricky to work with in some instances and many people dislike the bitter aftertaste. Some of the recipes could be adapted to use saccharin and still turn out well—others would not. An interesting note: just because an item is made without sugar, it is not necessarily low in calories. Some dietetic cakes, cookies and ice cream are just as high in calories as their non-dietetic counterparts. Check the labels.

Sugars all differ to some degree, but the end product is still the same—glucose, which is the simple sugar our bodies use for fuel.

So, with these few words of explanation and, perhaps, caution, enjoy the recipes in this chapter—in moderation!!

Fresh Fruit Plate

2 small apples,
  sliced
2 small oranges,
  peeled and
  sectioned
½ small banana,
  sliced
  lemon juice from
  ½ of a lemon
  mixed in I cup
  cold water

I cup Fruit Salad
Dressing (page 57)

1. Dip the apple and banana slices in the lemon water. (this keeps them from turning brown)

2. Arrange sliced apples, orange sections and banana slices alternately on 4 dessert plates.

3. Top each with ¼ cup of Fruit Salad Dressing.

4. Garnish each with an orange slice or a sprig of fresh mint.

Makes 4 servings.

Each serving contains:

180 calories
  8 grams protein
30 grams carbohy-
  drate
  4 grams fat
10 mgs. cholesterol

156 mgs. sodium
  3 grams dietary
  fiber
ADA Exchange Value
  I Lean Meat
  2 Fruit

Peaches and Chutney

These are a colorful and tasty accompaniment to
Mediterranean or Indian food. They are also good
served with sliced ham or roast chicken.

2 medium peaches,
  unpeeled
4 tablespoons Judy's
  Chutney (page
  136)

1. Preheat oven to 350 degrees.

2. Halve peaches and remove stone.

3. Place in a pie pan or baking dish.

4. Top each with 1 tablespoon Chutney.

5. Bake for 10 minutes.

6. Serve hot or cold.

Makes 4 servings.

Each serving contains:

35 calories	0 mgs. cholesterol
0 grams protein	1 mg. sodium
9 grams carbohy-drate	2 grams dietary fiber
0 grams fat	**ADA Exchange Value**
	½ Fruit

Apricot Pudding

3 1-pound cans wa-
  ter packed apricot
  halves
2 envelopes unfla-
  vored gelatin
1 orange

2 packets Equal
  (or 2 teaspoons
  fructose)
¼ cup walnuts,
  chopped

1. Drain apricots, reserve 1 cup liquid.

2. Heat liquid to boiling, pour over gelatin, stir until dissolved.

3. Mix juice from the orange with Equal.

4. Add juice to apricots and place mixture in a food processor with metal blade or in a blender and puree.

5. Add gelatin mixture to apricots, blend well.

6. Pour into a mold or bowl and chill until set (several hours).

7. To serve, unmold or spoon into small bowls, garnish with chopped walnuts.

Makes 6 servings.

Each serving contains:

111 calories
  4 grams protein
 18 grams carbohy-
     drate
  3 grams fat
  0 mgs. cholesterol

10 mgs. sodium
 4 grams dietary
   fiber
ADA Exchange Value
 1 Fruit
 1 Fat

Strawberries in a Cloud

This dessert is delicious and light and can be made with any fresh fruit.

Meringues:
- 2 egg whites
- 1 ¼ tablespoons fructose

Sauce:
- 2 cups nonfat milk
- 4 teaspoons arrowroot
- 1 tablespoon fructose
- 2 tablespoons Contreau or Triple Sec
- 1 pint fresh strawberries, hulled and halved

1. Beat egg whites until frothy. Gradually add fructose and continue beating to stiff peaks.

2. Heat milk in a 10" skillet to just before boiling point.

3. Drop 4 large spoonfuls of meringue into milk.

4. Poach for 2 minutes, then carefully turn and poach for 2 minutes on the other side.

5. Remove carefully with a slotted spoon to a flat dish.

6. Mix arrowroot, fructose, and Contreau in a small bowl.

7. Gradually add mixture to steaming milk, stirring constantly until thickened.

8. Pour into a bowl and chill about 30 minutes.

9. To serve, divide sauce equally into 4 dessert bowls, top with poached meringue and strawberries.

Makes 4 servings.

Each serving contains:

- 121 calories
- 6 grams protein
- 22 grams carbohydrate
- 0 grams fat
- 2 mgs. cholesterol
- 90 mgs. sodium
- 2 grams dietary fiber

ADA Exchange Value
- 1 Fruit
- ½ Nonfat Milk

Brown Rice Pudding

2 cups short grain brown rice, cooked

½ cup raisins, chopped

6 egg whites, slightly beaten

¼ cup fructose

1 can evaporated skimmed milk

1 teaspoon vanilla

1 teaspoon cinnamon

nutmeg

1. Preheat oven to 325 degrees.

2. Spray a 10" baking dish with a nonstick spray. Combine rice and chopped raisins.

3. Mix egg whites and fructose.

4. Add milk, vanilla, and cinnamon, mix well.

5. Pour mixture over rice and raisins.

6. Sprinkle liberally with nutmeg.

7. Place baking dish in a large pan half filled with water.

8. Bake for 1 hour or until set in the center.

Makes 8 servings.

One serving = 1 cup.

Each serving contains:

145 calories

6 grams protein

30 grams carbohydrate

0 grams fat

1 mg. cholesterol

100 mgs. sodium

1 gram dietary fiber

ADA Exchange Value

1 Starch/Bread

1 Fruit

Chocolate Souffle

¼ cup fructose
3 tablespoons cornstarch
3 tablespoons imported cocoa powder, unsweetened
1 teaspoon instant coffee

¼ teaspoon cinnamon
1 can evaporated skimmed milk
1 teaspoon vanilla
2 egg whites

1. Combine fructose, cornstarch, cocoa powder, instant coffee and cinnamon in a 2 quart saucepan.

2. Add milk and cook over medium heat, stirring constantly until mixture comes to a boil and thickens.

3. Add vanilla.

4. Pour into a 1 quart bowl and cover surface of pudding with waxed paper to prevent "skin" formation.

5. Chill for 1 hour.

6. Beat egg whites until stiff.

7. Fold into chocolate mixture until fully incorporated.

8. Spoon into individual 4 ounce dessert dishes.

Makes 4 servings.

Each servings contains:

205 calories
9 grams protein
28 grams carbohydrate
7 grams fat
25 mgs. cholesterol

116 mgs. sodium
0 grams dietary fiber
ADA Exchange Value
1½ Starch/Bread
½ Nonfat Milk
1 Fat

Rum Custard

2 whole eggs
2 egg whites
2 cups nonfat milk
1 tablespoon
  fructose

1 ½ teaspoons rum
  flavoring

1. Preheat oven to 350 degrees.

2. Beat whole eggs and egg whites slightly in a bowl.

3. Add the rest of ingredients and mix well.

4. Pour into 4 custard cups.

5. Place custard cups in a baking dish and fill halfway up with water.

6. Bake for 50 minutes, or until a knife inserted in center of custard comes out clean.

Makes 4 servings.

Each serving contains:

102 calories
9 grams protein
10 grams carbohy-
   drate
3 grams fat
139 mgs. cholesterol

122 mgs. sodium
0 grams dietary
  fiber
ADA Exchange Value
1 Medium - Fat
  Meat
½ Nonfat Milk

Tapioca Pudding

2 cups nonfat milk
4 tablespoons quick cooking tapioca
3 tablespoons fructose

1 teaspoon vanilla
2 egg whites

1. Combine milk, tapioca and 2 tablespoons fructose in a 2 quart saucepan and let stand for 5 minutes.

2. Heat milk mixture over medium heat, stirring constantly until it comes to a boil.

3. Remove from heat, add vanilla and allow to cool for ½ hour.

4. Beat egg whites until foamy, slowly add 1 tablespoon fructose and beat to soft peaks.

5. Fold cooled tapioca into egg whites.

Makes 6 servings.

Each serving contains:

78 calories
4 grams protein
15 grams carbohydrate
0 grams fat
1 mg. cholesterol

59 mgs. sodium
0 grams dietary fiber
ADA Exchange Value
½ Starch/Bread
½ Nonfat Milk

Lemon Cheese Pie

Crust:
- 2 teaspoons corn oil margarine
- 4 graham cracker squares
- ½ teaspoon allspice
- ½ teaspoon lemon peel

Filling:
- 2 cups lowfat cottage cheese
- ¼ cup fructose
- 2 teaspoons vanilla
- 1 teaspoon lemon peel
- 1 teaspoon fresh lemon juice

Topping:
- ¾ cup sour cream
- 2 tablespoons fructose
- 1½ teaspoons vanilla

1. Preheat oven to 375 degrees.

2. Put graham crackers, allspice, and lemon peel in a food processor or blender and blend into crumbs.

3. Melt margarine and slowly pour into the graham cracker crumbs while blender is running.

4. Place crumbs in a 9" pie plate that has been sprayed with a nonstick spray, and press down with finger tips evenly.

5. Put cottage cheese, fructose, vanilla, lemon peel and lemon juice in a food processor or blender and blend until smooth.

6. Pour cottage cheese mixture into the graham cracker shell.

7. Bake for 15 minutes.

8. While pie is baking combine topping ingredients in a mixing bowl and mix thoroughly.

9. Remove pie from oven and spread topping evenly over the top.

10. Place back in the oven and continue baking for 10 minutes.

11. Cool to room temperature then refrigerate until chilled before serving.

Makes 8 servings.

Each serving contains:

153 calories
9 grams protein
15 grams carbohy-
drate
7 grams fat
14 mgs. cholesterol

269 mgs. sodium
0 grams dietary
fiber
ADA Exchange Value
1 Starch/Bread
1 Medium-Fat Meat

Cake Roll

This is a basic cake roll that you can roll up with a variety of fillings including low calorie jelly and preserves for the traditional jelly roll.

**¾ cup unbleached
    pastry flour, sifted
¾ teaspoon baking
    powder
  2 whole eggs**

**3 egg whites
2 tablespoons
    fructose
¼ teaspoon vanilla**

1. Preheat oven to 400 degrees.

2. Line a 11x16x½ jelly roll pan with waxed paper and spray with a nonstick spray.

3. Sift together flour and baking powder.

4. Whip whole eggs until fluffy, gradually add fructose and vanilla and beat until very light and thick.

5. Fold flour mixture into eggs.

6. Spread evenly on jelly roll pan and bake 8 to 9 minutes or until cake springs back when pressed lightly in the center.

7. Let cake cool 2 to 3 minutes, then turn out onto a tea towel that has been lightly floured.

8. Remove wax paper (if cake is dry and crisp around edges, trim them.

9. Roll the cake in the tea towel and let cool.

10. When you are ready to fill the cake, unroll, but do not flatten edges, spread with your filling and re-roll using the towel to help you.

11. Chill at least 2 hours before slicing.

Makes 12 servings.

Each serving contains:

51 calories
3 grams protein
8 grams carbohy-
   drate
1 gram fat

48 mgs. cholesterol
45 mgs. sodium
0 grams dietary
   fiber
ADA Exchange Value
½ **Starch/Bread**

Chocolate Roll

Use ½ cup unbleached pastry flour with ¼ cup cocoa.
Increase fructose to ½ cup and vanilla to 1 teaspoon.

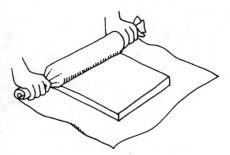

Black Forest Roll

1 envelope gelatin
¼ cup boiling water
1 cup skimmed evaporated milk, very cold
1 tablespoon imported cocoa powder
1 teaspoon instant coffee

½ teaspoon vanilla
1 tablespoon fructose, or 2 packets Equal
20 black cherries, pitted
1 Chocolate Cake Roll (page 153)

1. Add boiling water to gelatin, stir until dissolved, set aside.

2. Whip chilled milk in a cold bowl with cold beaters until double in volume.

3. Add cocoa, instant coffee, vanilla and fructose or Equal, while whipping.

4. Slowly pour in gelatin. Whip until slightly thick.

5. Put in refrigerator 15 minutes. Take out and stir (you don't want a lot of air in it).

6. Spread on Chocolate Cake Roll.

7. At the beginning of the roll, put a row of cherries.

8. Roll up the roll and refrigerate at least 2 hours before slicing.

Makes 12 servings.

Each serving contains:

104 calories
5 grams protein
18 grams carbohydrate
1 gram fat
46 mgs. cholesterol

71 mgs. sodium
0 grams dietary fiber
ADA Exchange Value
1 Starch/Bread

Upside Down Apple Gingerbread

2 cups unbleached all purpose flour, sifted

1 ¾ teaspoons ground ginger

1 ¼ teaspoon ground cinnamon

¼ teaspoon ground cloves

2 teaspoons baking powder

¼ teaspoon baking soda

¼ cup corn oil margarine

⅓ cup fructose

2 egg whites

1 cup nonfat milk

⅓ cup molasses

1 apple, cored and thinly sliced

1. Preheat oven to 350 degrees.

2. Sift together flour, ginger, cinnamon, cloves, baking powder and baking soda.

3. Beat margarine and fructose together.

4. Add egg whites and beat until light and fluffy.

5. Combine milk and molasses.

6. Add milk mixture and flour mixture alternately to margarine mixture until all is well blended.

7. Spray a tube pan with a nonstick spray.

8. Put a layer of apple around the pan.

9. Pour batter over the apple.

10. Bake 45 minutes or until done. (When a toothpick comes out clean.)

11. Let stand 5 minutes, then turn onto a serving plate.

12. Serve hot or cold.

Makes 12 servings.

Each serving contains:

165 calories	*139 mgs. sodium*
3 grams protein	*1 gram dietary fiber*
29 grams carbohy-	***ADA Exchange Value***
drate	*1 ½ Starch/Bread*
4 grams fat	*½ Fruit*
0 mgs. cholesterol	*½ Fat*

No Bake Cheese Cake

Crust:
- 6 graham crackers, crushed
- 1 teaspoon dry Butter Buds
- 2 teaspoons margarine melted
- ½ teaspoon orange peel

Filling:
- 2 envelopes gelatin
- ½ cup fructose
- 1 egg yolk
- 1 6 ounce frozen orange juice concentrate, thawed
- 3 cups lowfat cottage cheese
- 2 egg whites
- 1 cup skimmed evaporated milk, chilled

1. Mix graham crackers with Butter Buds, margarine and orange peel. Reserve ¼ cup for garnish. Put the rest of the crumbs in the bottom of a spring form pan and press in place.

2. Mix gelatin, fructose, egg yolk and orange juice into top of a double boiler.

3. Cook over boiling water, stirring constantly until gelatin dissolves and mixture thickens (about 10 minutes).

4. Remove from heat and cool.

5. Whip cottage cheese in food processor or blender until smooth.

6. Add gelatin mixture to cottage cheese and refrigerate until mixture mounds slightly, stir occasionally.

7. Beat egg whites until stiff, set aside.

8. Beat skimmed evaporated milk in a cold bowl with cold beaters until volume has increased five times (it will look like whipped cream).

9. Fold egg whites and whipped milk into gelatin mixture.

10. Pour into crust line pan, sprinkle with reserved crumbs.

11. Refrigerate several hours.

12. To serve, release spring on pan and gently lift off sides. Cut into pie shaped wedges, garnish with orange slices.

Makes 12 servings.

Each serving contains:

147 calories
11 grams protein
20 grams carbohy-
    drate
 3 grams fat
26 mgs. cholesterol

296 mgs. sodium
  0 grams dietary
    fiber
ADA Exchange Value
  1 Medium-Fat Meat
  1 Fruit
 ½ Nonfat Milk

Coffee

COFFEE—YOUR CHOICES

Coffee is the symbol of hospitality the world over. A quote from Francis Bacon, 17th century: "They have in Turkey a drink called coffee. This drink comforteth the brain and heart and helpeth digestion."

We agree: there is nothing quite like a "good" cup of coffee. In the past 10 years, many coffee stores have opened where a wide variety of different coffees are available. Happily, in the past couple of years a larger choice of decaffeinated coffee, rich with flavor, has been appearing, too. Even supermarkets are carrying whole beans which can be ground at purchase or taken home if you have a coffee grinder.

To keep your coffee fresh, store in an airtight container in your refrigerator or freezer. If you keep different blends, be sure to label them. When you venture into a store that specializes in coffee, plan to spend some time talking to the clerk about the different blends. This will help you choose the right ones for your tastes and needs.

Here are a few of our favorites and ones we have used in our menu planning. All are decaffeinated.

BREAKFAST COFFEE... A good full-bodied morning coffee can be Mocha Java, or Viennese. If you like a lighter tasting coffee, try Colombian. To get the most flavor out of the bean without the bitterness, use a drip method of preparation. Melita-style coffee makers, using the cone-shape filter, make a quick and wonderful cup or pot. For a change, add an inch of vanilla bean or ½ teaspoon ground cinnamon to the beans before brewing.

AFTERNOON COFFEE.....Iced coffee can be a real afternoon treat. With a bit of nonfat milk and some sweetener it tastes like dessert! To make good iced coffee, brew coffee double strength and pour over ice cubes in tall glasses (the extra strong coffee allows for the dilution caused by the ice). Or, brew extra breakfast coffee and freeze into coffee ice cubes. Then make iced coffee anytime by pouring regular strength coffee over the cubes.

AFTER DINNER COFFEE....Good types of coffee for after dinner are Espresso, French, Viennese, Java, Mocha or Mocha Java. These can all be found in decaffeinated beans. You might want to make your own special house blend. Our favorite method of brewing after dinner coffee is with a Melior-type pot. Pour the boiling water on the beans, let steep, then plunge down again. You're not boiling it, which can give it a bitter flavor. The pot not only looks nice on your table, but is a good conversation piece. Few people are aware of them (though they are widely used throughout Europe). Serve your after dinner coffee in demitasse cups. When making Espresso, serve it with some lemon peel on the side or the essence of anise in it.

CAPPUCCINO...Whip 1 cup evaporated skimmed milk with 2 teaspoons of sweetener or 1 packet Equal and ½ teaspoon vanilla. Fill a coffee cup halfway with whipped milk and pour Espresso over it.

TURKISH COFFEE...Use very fine or pulverized coffee. Mocha or Mocha Java are good ones to use. (If you have a coffee grinder, just grind the coffee twice as long. If you don't have a grinder, ask the clerk at the coffee store to do it for you.)

Coffee

To make 4 demitasse cups:
1½ cups water
3 tablespoons coffee with ⅛ teaspoon ground coriander
1 tablespoon sweetener or 2 packets Equal
   Bring water to boil in a saucepan or a pot designed for making Turkish coffee. (These can be found at a coffee specialty store.) Add coffee and coriander. Allow coffee to come to a boil and froth up twice. Take it off heat each time to allow it to go back down. Stir in sweetener or Equal and allow to froth up once more. Pour into demitasse cups.

MOCHA COFFEE...Fill coffee cup ½ with coffee and ½ with hot cocoa.*

*HOT COCOA...Mix 2 teaspoons cocoa with 2 teaspoons sweetener or 1 packet Equal and 1 tablespoon hot water. Stir in 2 cups hot, nonfat milk. Makes 2 cups.

Definitions

BAKE—Cook in heated oven.

BARBECUE—Cook over hot coals.

BASTE—To spoon or brush liquid over food while cooking.

BEAT—Mix foods or liquids vigorously with a spoon, whip or electric beater.

BLANCH—Dip food quickly in boiling water.

BLEND—Combine two or more ingredients less vigorously than beating.

BOIL—Heat liquid until constantly bubbling.

BROIL—Cook under broiler element.

CHOP—Cut pieces of food ⅛ to ½ inch squared (using a knife or food processor).

COAT—Roll or shake food to cover it.

CODDLE, EGGS—Put whole egg (in shell) in boiling water—30 seconds.

COOL—Allow to stand at room temperature until cool to the touch.

CORE—Remove core from fruits.

CRUSH—Crush dry herbs with mortar and pestle before using (or rub between your hands) to release flavor.

DEGLAZE—After food has been roasted or sauteed, a liquid is poured into pan, releasing crusted and flavorful juices or drippings.

FOLD IN—Using a rubber spatula in a circular motion, coming across the bottom and folding the bottom of the mixture over the top until the ingredients are mixed thoroughly but gently.

JULIENNE CUT—Cut in strips approximately ¼ inch by 2 inches.

MARINATE—Allow food to sit in marinade 2 to 24 hours as indicated.

MINCE—Chop very finely.

POACH—Cook for short time in simmering liquid.

PRE-HEAT—Set oven to temperature desired 5 to 10 minutes before using.

REDUCE—Boil down liquid, reducing it in quantity and concentrating taste.

ROAST—Bake uncovered meat or poultry.

SAUTE—Cook in small amount of oil or reduced stock in a skillet.

SEED—Completely remove small seeds from such foods as tomatoes, cucumbers, bell peppers.

SIFT—Put flour and other dry ingredients through a sifter.

SIMMER—Cook just below boiling point.

SNIP—Cut into small pieces using scissors or kitchen shears.

STIFFLY BEATEN—Beat until mixture stands in stiff peaks.

STIR—Mix with a spoon until all ingredients are well blended.

WHIP—Beat rapidly with fork, whisk, egg beater or electric mixer to add air and increase volume of mixture.

ABOUT THE AUTHORS

*J*udy Gilliard and Joy Kirkpatrick are a perfectly paired partnership. Together, they have used bushels of imagination and a delightfully fresh approach to healthful food preparation.

Judy, who holds a degree in restaurant management, has been a restaurant consultant and an instructor in the same field. She is trained in classical French methods of cuisine. A few years ago, Judy was diagnosed as a diet-controlled (type II) diabetic. Her diet "prescription" included a low-fat, low-salt, low-cholesterol regimen. She was encouraged to include fresh fruits, vegetables and whole grain products in her diet.

Judy was faced with new dietary requirements, and the knowledge that her health and daily well-being depended on these requirements. She met and consulted with Joy Kirkpatrick, a registered dietitian, specializing in diabetes education since 1976. Joy had worked at Eisenhower Medical Center's Diabetes Education Program, in Rancho Mirage, California, and at Palm Springs Medical Center in Palm Springs, California.

Trained in the art of, and still loving gourmet cooking, Judy set out to find ways to make her diet taste exciting and anything but bland.

Stating that she'd always wanted to write cookbooks, Judy then spoke with Joy about collaborating on a cookbook for health-conscious people.

From that simple idea springs this wonderful book of delicious, gourmet recipes that everyone can, and will enjoy. The best of their recipes are presented here for dieters, diabetics, individuals on sodium- or cholesterol-restricted diets and for anyone interested in sound nutrition and creative cookery!

When not working on recipes for **THE GUILTLESS GOURMET,** Joy spends her time in private practice as a consultant to various facilities and programs in Southern California's Coachella Valley. She is a member of both the American Dietetic Association and the American Diabetes Association. She was on the editorial committee for the revision of the American Diabetes Association cookbook, has taught nutrition at the community college level, participated in numerous seminars in weight control and the importance of diet in good health maintenance. She has contributed articles to *Forecast Magazine.*

Judy is Vice President/General Sales Manager for KPSI Radio Corporation in Palm Springs, California. She also adds to her credentials a membership with the American Food and Wine Institute.

Index

Recipe Notes

Recipe Notes

Recipe Notes

Recipe Notes

Recipe Notes

If you found this book helpful and would like more information on this and other related subjects you may be interested in one or more of the following titles from our *Wellness and Nutrition Library.*

BOOKS:

The Joy of Snacks — Good Nutrition for People Who Like to Snack (288 pages)

The Physician Within (210 pages)

Pass The Pepper Please (90 pages)

Fast Food Facts (40 pages)

Convenience Food Facts (137 pages)

Opening The Door To Good Nutrition (186 pages)

Learning To Live Well With Diabetes (392 pages)

Exchanges For All Occasions (210 pages)

A Guide To Healthy Eating (60 pages)

BOOKLETS & PAMPHLETS

Diabetes & Alcohol (4 pages)

Diabetes & Exercise (20 pages)

Emotional Adjustment To Diabetes (16 pages)

Healthy Footsteps For People With Diabetes (13 pages)

Diabetes Record Book (68 pages)

Diabetes & Brief Illness (8 pages)

Diabetes & Impotence: A Concern for Couples (6 pages)

Adding Fiber To Your Diet (10 pages)

Gestational Diabetes: Guidelines for A Safe Pregnancy and Healthy Baby (24 pages)

Recognizing and Treating Insulin Reactions (4 pages)

Hypoglycemia (functional) (4 pages)

The *Wellness and Nutrition Library* is published by Diabetes Center, Inc. in Minneapolis, Minnesota, publishers of quality educational materials dealing with health, wellness, nutrition, diabetes and other chronic illnesses. All our books and materials are available nationwide and in Canada through leading bookstores. If you are unable to find our books at your favorite bookstore contact us directly for a free catalog:

Diabetes Center, Inc.
P.O. Box 739
Wayzata, MN 55391